Best
Tom Kirkpatrick

The Love that Endures

Remembering my Mother and my
Father, USS Arizona's Chaplain at
Pearl Harbor

The Love that Endures

Remembering my Mother and my Father, USS Arizona's Chaplain at Pearl Harbor

Thomas I. Kirkpatrick

Greenbrier Publications - Half Moon Bay California

Copyright © 2011, Thomas I. Kirkpatrick. All rights reserved. Except for brief quotations in critical articles or reviews, no part of this book may be reproduced without prior written permission from the publisher.

Greenbrier Publications, 16 Greenbrier Court, Half Moon Bay, California, 94019

Hardback: 978-1-105-03066-6
Paperback: 978-1-105-13166-0

Dedicated to my parents,

Thomas LeRoy Kirkpatrick and Genevieve Burnet Kirkpatrick;

to the military families, both past and present,

whose many sacrifices keep our freedoms safe;

to the Arizona survivors I was privileged to meet

who told me their stories, often with difficulty

as they relived painful experiences of suffering and loss;

and to the chaplains of all faiths

who minister to the needs of our

fighting men and women,

sometimes giving up their own

lives in service to God and Country.

Acknowledgments

Richard Rhodes, Pulitzer-Prize-winning author of *The Making of the Atomic Bomb*, recounts in another of his books, *How to Write*, that his first boss gave him an invaluable piece of advice when he was young. Rhodes had been struggling to become an author, without much success. He asked his boss, a man named Conrad Knickerbocker, how he had managed to work full time and also write a number of successful books. The answer: "Rhodes, you apply a** to chair!" Rhodes calls this Knickerbocker's Rule.

While Knickerbocker's Rule most certainly applies—no pun intended—I believe that no author writes a significant work all by himself, just sitting there typing away. In child rearing, the expression "It takes a village" has become popular in recent years. I believe it applies to writing as well. My village is called Senior Coastsiders Writers' Workshop. For several years I have attended the weekly meetings of this group, listening to my fellow writers read their latest efforts to each other and in return receive helpful critiques, encouragement, and support. Along the way, I have heard some wonderful stories, each told in the unique voice of the author, some of them so touchingly personal and heartfelt they literally bring listeners to tears.

The leader of the group, Suzanne Black, offers us her solid wisdom and experience in writing and publishing. She is the glue that holds us together and keeps us on the right path. I have benefited enormously from her wise counsel and leadership as well as from the feedback my fellow writers have given me. I offer my sincere thanks. I couldn't have done it without them.

Over the years, various members of my large, extended family have shared their memories of their favorite Uncle Roy and Aunt Genevieve. Many of them knew about the boxes I had inherited that were filled with my parents' letters and photographs. Their question, oft repeated, was, "When are you going to write the book about them?" Their sincere interest served as a constant reminder that I had a family obligation. However, it was always something I intended to get around to one of these days. You know how that is, I'm sure.

It was my wife, Cecilia Anne Kirkpatrick, who first started browsing through the boxes of letters. One day she said to me, "You've talked about writing a book about the love story of your friends Adalberto and Dina Viggiano." And I had, because we recently had attended a memorial for Adalberto. During the final year of his life, as a precious gift to his family, he had written down his memories of how he and Dina had met in war-torn Italy, married, emigrated to America, raised a large and close-knit family, and made a wonderful life here. His family read his writings during the memorial, and I was struck by the thought that their story would make a wonderful memoir. Then Cecilia said, "Have you read these letters between your mother and father? They're amazing! There's your love story. You just have to write it."

And so, I did.

Thomas I. Kirkpatrick

Preface

I wrote this book to tell a real love story about real people: my mother and father. They led a remarkable life together, full of the kinds of trials so many military families face today. My father's service as a Navy chaplain was marked by the usual periods of deployment aboard ship. While he was away, my mother "kept the home fires burning," as my father once wrote to her.

In these pages, I have tried to paint a picture of two people who loved each other deeply but who were forced to spend long periods apart. How did they keep their love alive and their marriage vibrant and fulfilling during these separations? As I began my research, one concept emerged: communication. It sounds trite, but it's the truth. Mother and Father really *worked* at staying in touch.

This story would not have been possible except for two things. First, both of my parents were committed letter writers, and secondly, after Father was killed during the Pearl Harbor attack, Mother carefully preserved the letters. She saved them over the years, carefully packing them in many boxes. How I wish I had paid attention. But this treasure trove lay waiting for someone to unearth and that someone turned out to be me.

I was still a young boy when Father died. As a result, I have precious few memories of him, what kind of a person he was, even how his voice sounded. The research for this book consisted largely of spending countless hours reading every single one of the hundreds of letters my mother and father had exchanged, many of them intensely personal and intimate. As I read, a picture of my father materialized for the first time. As an added bonus, a new and much more complete picture of my mother emerged as well.

When you read the excerpts of the letters, one thing is striking. The expression of romantic sentiment you would expect from two lovers is obvious, but there is also an amazing amount of mundane, ordinary, day-to-day talk. You can almost hear them as they sit down after dinner and tell each other about their day. That was their secret. They shared their lives fully with each other in their daily exchange of letters.

Of course, I can't forget the fact that my mother and father lived through and were directly involved in some of the most momentous events of the twentieth century. Father served in World War I in France, and later both he and Mother spent two years in Asia during the bloody and brutal Chinese Revolution. During the years between the two great wars, Father served aboard the first of the so-called fast aircraft carriers, the USS *Saratoga*, whose mission was to develop the naval air tactics that were so crucial to America's later victory in the Pacific. And finally, he was the first chaplain to give his life for his country in World War II.

Contents

ILLUSTRATIONS

Chapter 7

Chapter 8

Chapter 9

CHAPTER 1

Day of Infamy

"We interrupt this program to bring you a special news bulletin. The Japanese have attacked Pearl Harbor, Hawaii, by air, President Roosevelt has just announced. The attack also was made on all Naval and Military activities on the principal island, Oahu."

Time stood still as the urgent voice stunned Mother and me. We had been sitting in the small living room of our apartment in Webster Groves, Missouri, that pleasant Sunday afternoon listening to the regular broadcast from Columbia Broadcasting System when the announcer had broken in.

My father, Captain Thomas LeRoy Kirkpatrick, was the fleet chaplain aboard the USS *Arizona* (fig. 1-1), flagship of the battleship flotilla stationed at Pearl Harbor. The United States Navy's Pacific Fleet had been home ported there more than a year earlier to act as an advance line of defense against the increasingly warlike actions of Japan. Father would have been preparing for morning church services at just about that hour. Sick with apprehension, we sat listening for more news. The afternoon wore on, the announcer occasionally interrupting the regular programming with more fragments of information. As the reports came over the air, the picture grew worse and worse.

That Sunday morning, the fleet at anchor in the protected confines of Pearl Harbor had been going about its normal business. As the first wave of Japanese aircraft swept across the calm waters of the bay, sailors aboard *Arizona* and other ships were amazed to see the "meatball" painted on the wings of aircraft they had at first assumed to be American. They knew what that symbol meant. They were under attack. Shortly after 7:55 a.m. Hawaii time, *Arizona* sounded the air raid alarm. My father would have interrupted his church preparations and started to make his way to his assigned battle station, sick bay, where his duties were to assist in treating the wounded and to minister to the dying.

Mother and I went to bed that night not knowing the fate of my father or of his ship. The next day the entire nation was in a frenzy with the talk of outright war. President Roosevelt addressed Congress that day, beginning his speech:

> *"Yesterday, December 7, 1941—a date which will live in infamy—the United States of America was suddenly and deliberately attacked by naval and air forces of the Empire of Japan."*

The president asked for—*demanded* in his righteous wrath—a Declaration of War, which was quickly granted with but a single dissenting vote.

Late that same afternoon we heard a knock. Mother opened the apartment door to see a Western Union courier. With a sinking heart, she took the telegram, opened it, read it, and then without a word handed it to me.

DEAR MRS KIRKPATRICK STOP I REGRET TO INFORM YOU THAT YOUR HUSBAND CAPTAIN THOMAS LEROY KIRKPATRICK IS MISSING IN ACTION AND PRESUMED DEAD STOP SIGNED SECRETARY OF THE NAVY FRANK KNOX STOP

I was just old enough to know that death meant my father would not be coming home to us.

That night, as I climbed into bed and prepared to say my bedtime prayers, I asked Mother a childish question: "Mommy, should I leave Daddy out of my prayers now?"

Mother, with tears streaming down her face, replied softly, "No, Tommy. You must always keep Daddy in your prayers."

The next day we heard another knock on our door. Mother, still barely able to keep the tears from coursing down her cheeks, called out, "Who is it?"

A man's voice answered, brusque and businesslike, "Are you the Mrs. Kirkpatrick whose husband was killed in the Jap attack? I'm a reporter for the Webster Groves paper and I *must* talk to you."

Mother, appalled at this callous insensitivity to our grief and need for privacy answered querulously, "I can't talk to you now." To her dismay, the man persisted, banging on the door and demanding an interview. Mother began to cry, calling to him, "Please! Go away! I can't talk to you." I sat across the room, terrified, not knowing what to do. After many minutes, Mother took her bedside portrait of my father (fig. 1-2) out of its leather frame and slipped it beneath the door. The reporter took the picture and left without a word. The next edition of the local paper featured my father's portrait on the front page with huge black headlines blaring, "WEBSTER GROVES MAN KILLED IN JAP ATTACK." The story was filled with misinformation about my father mixed with fragmentary information about the attack itself. The portrait was never returned.

On January 2, 1942, Mother received an envelope bearing the return address "Secretary of the Navy, Washington—Official Business." Inside, as if to assuage the starkness of the earlier telegram, was a brief letter of condolence signed by Frank Knox himself (fig. 1-3). A year later Mother received a brief note of condolence, on a microfilm form known as V-mail, from Boatswains Mate Second Class Thomas W. Stanborough. At the time, he was serving aboard the USS *Leigh*, but he was one of the few eyewitness survivors among *Arizona's* crew who had been aboard her during the attack. He described seeing my father at the ship's stern rigging for church when the first bombs fell. According to other eyewitnesses, a brief moment after Seaman Stanborough saw my father, a bomb dropped from a Japanese "Kate" torpedo bomber, specially modified for high-altitude bombing glanced off the number four turret, the one closest to the ship's stern, and exploded on the deck where my father was last seen. Seconds later, a 1700-pound armor-piercing bomb penetrated the forward deck near the number two turret. It exploded four decks below, igniting the horrendous magazine explosion that literally tore the ship apart, killing nearly the entire crew (fig. 1-4).

In that moment, the twenty-year love affair between my mother and father tragically ended. Their love was the living embodiment of St. Paul's Letter to the Corinthians on Love:

> *Love is patient, love is kind. It is not jealous. Love does not brag and is not arrogant, does not act unbecomingly. It does not seek its own, is not provoked, does not take into account a wrong suffered, does not rejoice in unrighteousness but rejoices with the truth; bears all things, hopes all things, endures all things. But now abide faith, hope, love, these three; but the greatest of these is love.*

During their life together, Mother and Father endured many lengthy and stressful periods of separation due to my father's Navy service. The stresses of Navy life took their toll even during the times they were together during my father's shore duty. Through it all, my mother and father were faithful to each other and to the teachings of St. Paul to endure all things with and for each other.

This is the story of their inspiring and enduring love.

Fig. 1-1 U.S.S. Arizona The ship is shown here in her configuration at Pearl Harbor

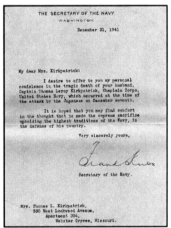

Fig. 1-2 Chaplain Thomas L. Kirkpatrick   *Fig. 1-3 Letter of condolence*

Fig. 1-4 Arizona's magazine exploding. Remarkable film
captured on 8mm film camera showing massive fireball.

CHAPTER 2

The Early Years

Thomas LeRoy Kirkpatrick was born in Cozad, Nebraska, on July 5, 1887, the youngest of five children. His family called him Roy. They moved to Colorado Springs, Colorado, while he was still young. He graduated from Colorado Springs High School in 1905. Possessing a fine singing voice, he was an active member of their glee club. He then went to Westminster College in Denver for two years, transferred to Colorado College in Colorado Springs for his junior and senior years, and graduated in 1911. He felt his pastoral calling early in life, long before being ordained as a Presbyterian minister. In school he took leadership roles in the Young Men's Christian Association (YMCA) where he was general secretary at the college his senior year.

He began his missionary work while in school, becoming the representative of the American Sunday School Union (ASSU) for Pueblo, Colorado. Still in college, he became an assistant pastor of a Presbyterian church in Colorado Springs. After graduation he applied to the ASSU for a position as a foreign missionary, and he was posted to their school in Tabriz, Persia. He thereupon embarked upon a five-week odyssey (fig. 2-1) from Denver to New York by train, across the Atlantic Ocean by steamer (fig. 2-2), across Europe by train, and across the Black Sea to Djulfa (now Tblisi) by tramp steamer (fig. 2-3). At that time, there was a virulent cholera epidemic raging that had killed fifty passengers on another ship, so the passengers on Tom's ship were forced to pass through quarantine stations where they were stripped and their clothes autoclaved (fig. 2-4). Finally came the last stage: the dangerous trek across the forbidding Caucasus Mountains by bus from Djulfa to Tabriz (fig. 2-5). Tom missed the Tuesday bus by a few hours, so took the Thursday bus, having spent the nights in a primitive Caravanserai while waiting. In fact, he barely missed possible death since the Tuesday bus had overturned in the mountains, killing several passengers.

After arriving safely in Tabriz, Tom lived and taught at the ASSU Memorial School for Boys (fig. 2-6) for three and a half years. At the time, Persia was trying unsuccessfully to fight off an armed invasion, during which Russian and Cossack armies shelled and stormed Tabriz, forcing everyone at the school to shelter in the basement while shells blew holes in the roof and windows. Thereafter, the conquerors instituted a reign of terror, with daily hangings becoming the norm (fig. 2-7). The missionaries did what they could to help the starving citizens of Tabriz during this trying time. Even in the midst of this turmoil and danger, Tom, being an avid people person and amateur photographer, traveled around the country, to the extent conditions allowed, taking hundreds of pictures of people and places (fig. 2-8, 2-9). Tom kept detailed diaries recording these events, including several harrowing escapes from danger.

Then in 1914, when the winds of war began blowing in Europe, Tom decided to return home, walking across the same forbidding Caucasus Mountains (fig. 2-10). He then retraced his path across the Middle East, Europe, and the Atlantic Ocean to the United States. Once back home, he realized a longstanding ambition by entering McCormick Theological Seminary where he was ordained in 1918. He decided to serve his country by applying for a commission in the Navy, graduating from Chaplains School in 1918 (fig. 2-11). During the final year of World War I, he was assigned to the High Power Radio Detachment in France, where he performed his chaplain's duties at the Navy's Lafayette Radio Station in Croix d'Hins.

After the armistice, he faced a major decision in his life. He could return to civilian life and become a church pastor, or he could continue as a Navy chaplain. He decided to remain faithful to what he had come to believe was his calling: ministering to the men of the Navy on land and at sea. Genevieve Burnet, soon to become his lifelong mate, later wrote that this was "a decision he never regretted, nor did I," in spite of the hardships and lengthy separations military life imposed.

His initial posting following the war was aboard the first of the Navy's modern so-called super-dreadnaughts, the USS *North Dakota* (fig. 2-12), where he served until July 13, 1921. He was then transferred to the USS *Utah* and took part in the ship's extended goodwill tour of numerous European and Mediterranean ports. Ever the enthusiastic photographer, he documented the ship's travels with hundreds of photographs, a few of which are shown here (fig. 2-13, 2-14). Naval vessels in those days were coal-fired, and Tom took pictures of a coaling operation, a slow and untidy business during which a ship called a collier would tie up alongside the vessel being coaled and, using huge clamshell scoops, would transfer tons of coal, trying not to scatter too much of the fuel around the deck. Invariably, the seamen of the ship would have to do major cleanup duty (fig. 2-15). At one point, even Tom, in spite of being an officer and chaplain, pitched in (fig. 2-16), an act that no doubt showed the ship's crew that their chaplain was no stuffed shirt, but a regular guy.

March 17, 1923, was a homecoming day for Lieutenant T. L. Kirkpatrick, Chaplain Corps, U.S.N. His ship, USS *Utah*, had just returned from her goodwill voyage. When his tour of duty aboard the Utah was finished, he was, to use the Navy parlance, detached from his duty as the ship's chaplain. He was ordered to shore duty at the Bureau of Navigation in Washington, D.C., where he reported on May 1, 1923, unaware of what fate had in store for him. He was about to meet his lifelong mate.

Genevieve McClenny Burnet (fig. 2-17), known as Janie to her family, was born in St. Louis on August 2, 1898, the youngest of six children. Her father, George Burnet III, was prominent in local politics and civic affairs. Being a civil engineer, he had designed and surveyed the Missouri Pacific Railroad right-of-way from St. Louis westward. Later, he was instrumental in building the magnificent St. Louis City Hall, a beautiful structure in the classic style that took fourteen years to complete, and still stands today (fig. 2-18). Its magnificent interior boasts marble floors and walls with an ornate gilded ceiling (fig. 2-19) supported by marble columns. An engraved granite tablet in the entryway of the building honors his memory by proclaiming his Presidency of the Board of Improvements, one of his many contributions to civic life. As a St. Louis selectman (like today's city councilman), he had laid out and gotten built a large part of the growing city's street grid.

Genevieve's mother, Annie McClenny Burnet, died when Genevieve was only six years old. Her father died when she was twelve. She was then raised by her eldest sister, Nan, who was married and lived with her husband, Wells Belding, on their farm outside St. Louis. Genevieve completed the eighth grade, and then her eldest brother, Leo, sent her to Chicago. He paid for her further education at a secretarial school. While still in her teens, she moved to the nation's capitol where she lived for a time in Bluemont, Virginia, with her cousins, Mr. and Mrs. Archibald A. Speer. She intended to apply for a civil service position. She passed the examination and was hired as a clerk/typist in the War Department, the predecessor to the modern day Department of Defense. By 1923, she had worked in this position for several years while living in Washington, D.C., at the Portland Hotel, a residence for respectable single ladies.

Genevieve believed fate had brought them both to Washington and to the War Department at the same point in time. It is not clear whether they first met at the War Department office building or at a D.C. social function, but the dashing young lieutenant, a chaplain, and the comely and well-bred young woman from a good family in St. Louis met, and both were smitten. She said many times over the years that she knew immediately he was *the* one. He courted her intently, in short order proposed, she accepted, and they started making plans for their wedding.

In the months before the wedding, during periods of separation, the couple exchanged correspondence attesting their love for each other. On her twenty-fifth birthday, he sent a small note (fig. 2-20) to her hotel, addressed to Miss Burnet, Apt. 64. It read simply and touchingly:

> *August second—to wish my true love a most happy birthday.*
>
> *Tom*

He enclosed a tiny red rose. She kept the note and dried blossom for the rest of her life.

In 1908, the YMCA of the Adirondacks had established a hotel and conference center known as the Silver Bay Association on Lake George, New York. Its purpose was to provide a place for religious workers to reaffirm their faith and renew their energies for their calling. On August 6, 1923, while on a religious retreat at Silver Bay, Tom sent a letter addressed to Miss Genevieve Burnet, Portland Hotel, 14th and Vermont NW, Washington, D.C. It read:

> *Sweetheart:*
>
> *I've been wishing all day you were with me, and especially this afternoon when I started up the lake on the boat. This is a wonderful spot, with clear sky above hills and mountains, which come down to the very edge of a crystal clear lake. Islands add more beauty and charm. I've just about decided that we ought to spend a few days at one of the many hotels up here....*
>
> *Worlds of love, Dearest,*
>
> *Tom*

In a P.S., he added simply, *"Twenty nine days."*

The couple married twenty-nine days later on September 5, 1923, in the garden of the Speers' home in Bluemont before a small group of friends. The officiating minister, Reverend E. H. Scott, began by reading the time-honored words in "The Order for the Solemnization of Marriage," taken from the *Book of Common Worship* of the Presbyterian Church. The words begin:

> *Dearly beloved, we are assembled here in the presence of God, to join this Man and this Woman in Holy Marriage; which is instituted of God, regulated by His commandments, blessed by our Lord Jesus Christ, and to be held in honour among all men.*

When the ceremony ended, Mr. and Mrs. Speer signed the small leather-bound Marriage Service book as witnesses (fig. 2-21). The eighteen close family friends in attendance signed also. The book, containing the sacred words they had spoken to each other, was so precious to Genevieve that she kept it carefully wrapped in tissue and safely stored away until her death in 1991 at age ninety-three.

Their wedding was the beginning of a lifetime of loving and supporting each other. Tom served the nation as a Navy chaplain, and Genevieve actively participated as his hostess and companion.

After their honeymoon, the newlyweds set up house in Washington, D.C., at 3501 Cathedral Avenue NW. Their at-home announcement invited friends to drop by after October 15, 1923. In November of 1924, while still on duty at the Bureau of Navigation in Washington, Tom was promoted to the rank of lieutenant commander. Then in September 1925, Tom's period of shore duty ended. He was ordered to report to the USS *Huron* (fig. 2-22), flagship of the Asiatic Fleet, at the Cavite Naval Station in the Philippine Islands. His new duty was to be fleet chaplain. In figure 2-23, he is seated on the left of the ship's commanding officer. Tom and Genevieve spent the next two years of their lives on the far side of the Pacific; sadly enough, most of the time separated from each other. Tom was aboard ship and at sea for great lengths of time. Genevieve lived briefly in the fleet's home port, Chefoo, China, then in Manila, and for a short time in Shanghai. Their marriage was sorely tested, and they realized the difficulties and hardships many military families faced. And yet, they found ways to keep their love alive. They worked hard to share the days of their lives through constant communication, even while forced apart by circumstances.

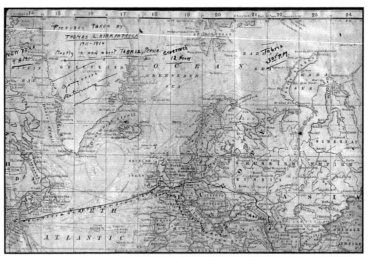

*Fig. 2-1 **The Oddysey*** Crosses mark the route going, dashes mark the route returning.

*Fig. 2-2 **North German Lines S.S. Kronprinz Wilhelm***

*Fig. 2-3 **Tramp Steamer in Catania, Sicily*** Across the Black Sea to Djulfa in this.

Fig. 2-4 Quarantine Station Autoclave. Passengers stripped, clothes autoclaved.

Fig. 2-5 Auto from Djulfa to Tabriz. Across rugged Caucasus Mountains in this.

Fig. 2-6 Tom at work in study at Memorial School for Boys, Tabriz.

Fig. 2-7 Hangings Cossack soldiers display their work to the citizens of Tabriz.

Fig. 2-8 Doing the wash Persian women cover faces while washing in street

Fig. 2-9 Leper in Tabriz   *Fig. 2-10 Road thru Caucasus Mtns.*

Fig. 2-11 Chaplain Class of 1918 Tom is the third from the right.

Fig. 2-12 U.S.S. North Dakota First of the Navy's "Superdreadnoughts."

Fig. 2-13 U.S.S. Utah's Goodwill tour Crew laying ceremonial honorary flowers.

*Fig. 2-14 **The tour guide*** Chaplains frequently acted as tour guides for sailors.

*Fig. 2-15 **Coaling Operation*** Slow, messy business. Crew performed cleanup duty.

*Fig. 2-16 **Even the chaplain helped.***   *Fig. 2-17 **Young Genevieve Burnet***

Fig. 2-18 Old St. Louis City Hall Pushed to completion by George Burnet III

Fig. 2-19 Ornate marble and guilded interior of Old City Hall

Fig. 2-20 Tom's birthday greeting Genevieve kept it all her life.

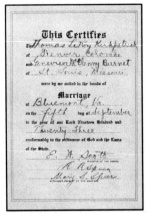

Fig. 2-21 Signed Marriage Book

Fig. 2-22 U.S.S. Huron in Chefoo Flagship of the Asiatic Fleet.

Fig. 2-23 Huron's Ships Company Chaplain seated at right of Captain.

CHAPTER 3

The Asiatic Tour

It is helpful to understand the tumultuous political situation in China during these years. The "powers," as Tom liked to refer to them, had trading and commercial interests in China during this period, and hence felt compelled to station military forces there to protect their interests and their citizens. The United States was prominent among the powers, which included players from the earlier so-called Eight-Nation Alliance, made up of Austria-Hungary, France, Germany, Italy, Japan, Russia, the United Kingdom, and the United States. The growing Chinese rebellion of the 1920s meant that the U.S. Asiatic Fleet was kept busy patrolling coastal waters, ferrying U.S. sailors and marines to trouble spots where American citizens needed help (fig. 3-1) and providing them with support.

The two major power centers driving the rebellion were the Kuo Mintang (later better known as the Chinese Nationalist Party), led by Chiang Kai-shek, and the Chinese Communist Party (CCP) under its charismatic leader Mao Tse-tung. Early in the decade, they had been allies, encouraged to get along by none other than Joseph Stalin. The Russians were stirring the pot by sending skilled operatives to the revolutionaries to provide organizational knowledge, financial aid, and even military advice and weaponry. Historians have written about the so-called Tragedy of the Revolution of 1925–27, instigated by the firebrand CCP leader in Canton, Chen Duxiu, an influential leader of the radical left-wing elements of the CCP. He was actively fomenting a rebellion-within-a-rebellion, in which he hoped to separate the CCP from its then-ally, the Kuo Mintang. His efforts ultimately proved successful, but fatal in the short run to his faction. Chiang stealthily plotted and staged a purge in which many hundreds of unfortunate CCP backers were killed in public beheadings and thousands more simply disappeared. Chiang then emerged in 1928 as the supreme leader of a united China, but this was only a temporary victory.

Initially Genevieve lived ashore in Chefoo, enjoying what must have been a rather pleasant life (fig. 3-2, 3-3), as did many other Navy wives. Life went on, with various social events, such as beach picnics (fig. 3-4). However, it was not long before the growing turmoil and brutal violence in China caused many among the military personnel of the Western powers to be concerned about the safety of their loved ones. Tom, along with most of his fellow U.S. Navy personnel, decided against having his family continue to live on the mainland. Genevieve moved into a rental home (fig. 3-5) in Manila, which was close to the Cavite Naval Base. Chefoo, the fleet's home port, was far north, placing it near the Korean Peninsula. From there, the fleet ranged up and down the eastern coast of China. However, Tom's ship occasionally visited places such as Hong Kong, where he and Genevieve could visit briefly (fig. 3-6). After one such rendezvous, he wrote:

11/17/26

Dearest:

... How I hated to see you steaming out alone! I was doubly "blue" last night.... This evening thirty pages in a book, and a few lines to send my love to my darling wife. Now to bed.

Night-night,

Tom

11/18/26

Another day and another night with its letter to you just before I turn in. I hope that you've happily arrived at the Lacey home by this, and that you're finding Manila comfortable and pleasant.... Now, to bed, with a good-night thought and prayer for you, my own darling wife.

All your own,

Tom

11/19/26

... I've been plugging away on my Thanksgiving sermon. I'm going to miss you on that day. It's our second one apart, isn't it? Maybe next one we'll be in a comfy California bungalow. Won't that be great? All my love.

Your own hubby,

Tom

Midway through his tour of duty in Asia, his ship, the USS *Huron*, was relieved as flagship by the heavy cruiser USS *Pittsburgh* (fig. 3-7), which arrived in Chefoo on December 23, 1926. Tom was transferred to the new flagship, still as the fleet chaplain. The new flagship continued to support the fleet's duty to protect U.S. interests and citizens from becoming victims of the extreme violence raging on the Chinese mainland.

Genevieve wrote to Tom almost daily during this period. She recounted the ins and outs of her daily life in Manila.

Sunday

Dearest Tommy:

One good thing about it, you won't get eaten up by mosquitoes in Shanghai. The little old house is mighty lonely. I walk around and it seems dead.... Old honey, if you don't come back here soon, I'll be up there, unless it is decidedly not advisable, for I don't like to be here alone. Don't forget to let me know if it is at all certain where you will be. Nighty night dear.

All my love,

Genevieve

Monday

Dear:

One day gone. Late breakfast again.... This afternoon I wrote checks and tore up papers, sorted receipts, and what not. Got them all off but the telephone bill—will have to pay the fifty centavos extra. Careless. Martha Thompson took me to the Monday Musical Club concert this afternoon. It was all very good. The stringed quartette was good—all Filipinos. They made me think of our Monday evening concerts at Central High, the New York Symphony ... wish we could go again.... All the folks call me the Merry Widow—don't know why. But I am going to entertain—it is too lonely by myself.

Tuesday

Tommy, Dear:

This afternoon I went down to see Agnes Ayres and Pat O'Malley in Tomorrow Love. *Have you seen it? It is rather funny in places. It starts with them signing the register at the hotel after their wedding. He signs "Mr. and Mrs. Robert Stanley and Wife." He at least didn't forget to register her name, as some people I know do.*

Oceans of love,

Genevieve

Her remark references a funny incident when Tom forgot to register in both their names, probably while on their honeymoon.

These letters illustrate Tom and Genevieve Kirkpatrick's personal history, and they also tell a story about the difficulties and hardships of military life: the long and agonizing separations, the extra burdens placed on military wives to run a household alone, even giving birth alone while husbands were away on duty as Genevieve did in 1932. Tom and Genevieve kept their marriage alive and vibrant through these daily letters to each other. They shared their feelings of love for each other, as well as the mundane events of their everyday lives. They worked hard to make each other feel as though they were sharing a life together, even though physically apart.

In January of 1927, the USS *Pittsburgh* sailed from Chefoo to Shanghai, escorting a contingent of 2,500 U.S. Marines and Sailors (fig. 3-8, 3-9) with orders to defend American citizens who might be in danger from the growing unrest and fighting between the warring factions of the Chinese revolution.

During that month, two letters crossed in the mail. Tom wrote from the USS *Pittsburgh* as the ship was delivering the troops to Shanghai.

1/13/27

Dearest:

Here it is after ten o'clock on the night of our arrival at Shanghai.... Things seem quiet here, though there are numerous ships present awaiting trouble, which everyone rather expects.... They all asked when you were coming up, but agreed that until something more definite is known as to the possibility of trouble here it is well for you to remain in Manila.... I spoke to a number of old friends who are on various ships here—the Asheville, Sacramento, Parrot, Peary, *and* McCormick.... *While I wish you were here, I am glad to have you where I'm not worried about you in case of trouble, so that's a big factor. I hope you are not too lonely in the house, and if you are that you'll close it up pronto and go to a hotel.*

...Well, honey, since I can't kiss you goodnight, all I can do is to send you heaps of love and kisses by mail, which I do.

Your own loving Hubby

The same day, she wrote:

1/13

Dearest Tommy:

I am tired but Mrs. Thompson is coming over in a few minutes to take me down to see the Madison *off. Some of the Pittsburgh wives expect to go to Shanghai unless they have heard from their husbands to the contrary today.... Time to go.*

Oodles of love,

Genevieve

Naval history archives tell us something of the fate of several of the ships Tom names, and aboard which he had friends. *Asheville* (fig. 3-10) was a patrol gunboat still stationed in Asian waters on December 7, 1941. She was sunk in March of 1942 in a pitched battle south of Java, severely outgunned by an enemy force consisting of a cruiser and two destroyers. She went down with the loss of nearly all hands. One of the few survivors reported that some were machine gunned by the Japanese while struggling in the water. The gunboat *Sacramento* (fig. 3-11) was in Pearl Harbor on December 7 and was credited with downing at least two of the attacking aircraft. The USS *Parrott* (fig. 3-12) took part in a successful torpedo attack on Japanese ships in Balikpapan Bay, Indonesia in January of 1942 and then served in the Atlantic until late in the war. The destroyer USS *Peary* (fig. 3-13) was damaged in air raids on Cavite early in the war, survived, and went on to perform heroic service while defending Darwin, Australia, from a massive air attack in February 1942. She was sunk with the loss of nearly one hundred of her crew after being struck by five bombs. Her machine gunners continued firing at the attackers even while the ship sank stern-first into Darwin Bay. The destroyer USS *McCormick* (fig. 3-14) was decommissioned in 1938, but recommissioned at the outbreak of hostilities in World War II. She served in the Atlantic on convoy escort and sub-hunting duties during the war.

On a personal note, Genevieve wrote a letter in January in which she made clear how anxious she was to start their family:

1/14/27

Dearest:

You should be in Shanghai by now. I am wondering what the conditions are—whether it is advisable for me to come up or not. Mr. Howard and Miss Bodham and I went out to the Tondo Convent to see their lace. It is exquisite. Of course I got some—four hankies, one lace and three linen with lace edge plus two lace baby pillow tops, two baby caps, and one baby's jacket. You see, I am getting ready for our family when we get home.... Well, I'm off to the Y now. Maybe a note afterward.

Love,

Genevieve

The convent she refers to still exists today as a part of Santo Nino de Tondo Parish in Manila, an ancient church dating from 1572.

After his ship had returned to Chefoo, Tom wrote letters that illustrate other trying aspects of military life, at least Navy life:

1/28/27

Dearest:

This is being written in rather a hurry, as the mail closes in a half hour, via the President Harrison. *I've just mailed you a check on the same post, registered, which I hope reaches you in safety. Sent one hundred fifty, which makes sufficient surplus to carry you through February, I hope.... Thus leaving you another $100 (US) coming from me for this February allowance (or shall we say salary?). I hope you'll make up the household accounts for the months of housekeeping, so that we'll know what it costs us to live in Manila. Can do? Meanwhile, if you do run short at any time, you have the Washington account to fall back on, though I hope we won't have to touch that. We're going to need that within the year.*

... I feel that so long as you can be content in Manila it is much wiser, until we know what is going to happen here. The first contingent of British troops and of French Colonials arrived yesterday and have their pictures in today's papers. Also, a statement from Eugene Chen, of the Canton Party, that the British will have to take the blame for whatever may now happen in or about Shanghai, which may be a threat of war or may be for its effect on the world's sympathy and a bid for that. He gets little from me at the present time, for until his party can show a bit more control and wisdom, they aren't ready for foreign cooperation without a certain amount of foreign control.

... All my love, old sweetheart. Hope you're well and happy and plans are going along smoothly. Let me know what you are doing about the house and furniture and so forth. Hope you can sell the stove and have that money to spend.

Heaps of love from your affectionate Hubby,

Tom

When Tom refers to Eugene Chen, he is talking about Chen Duxiu, who apparently used an Anglicized name when talking to the Western press.

In those days, the Navy, and possibly the other branches of the U.S. military, rarely provided such things as on-base housing for the so-called dependents. Most often this meant that the wives had to locate housing for themselves and their children in nearby civilian communities, arrange for moving in and setting up housekeeping, buy what they needed locally, and pay the bills. The Navy paid the men at their current duty station, possibly in cash. It was up to the individual service personnel to provide funds for their families, wherever they might be. Electronic funds transfer did not exist at this time, so Tom sent funds to Genevieve by registered mail carried on the President Lines' mail ships. Cell phones did not exist, and even landlines were rare, so people kept in touch by mail. The reference to *President Harrison* identifies the American President Lines mail ship, which was about to sail from Chefoo to points south. To avoid long delays, one had to pay particular attention to posted ship sailing and arrival schedules so as not to miss the "mail close" mentioned by Tom.

In a particularly heartfelt and intimate letter, Tom wrote to Genevieve from Chefoo expressing his frustration at their separation, his longing to be reunited with his bride, as well as his desire, shared with her, to start a family.

> *2/8/27*
>
> *Dearest:*
>
> *Did you learn a lot at the lecture on present conditions in China? He is indeed a rash person who would attempt to say just what they are, for things shift so rapidly.... Chen still seems to be talking in pretty strong terms, it seems to me, and I doubt whether the Powers will accept terms such as he sees fit to make. So don't buy your ticket yet, but don't give up your March steamer reservation.... I'm just as eager as can be for you to be with me, but so long as it is cold and disagreeable, with most everyone having severe colds, it isn't the most pleasant place to be, and should there be trouble, it would be even less pleasant.*

... The last roll of film had six good ones on it, so you see I am learning how to use it. It is an excellent camera, and we'll have many good photos with it—perhaps of the twins some day. How does that sound?

The lights are burning by your picture, darling girl, but that doesn't satisfy me. I want to hold you in my arms and tell you that I love you more than anyone else in the world. Can you hear me? I do. So just snuggle right up close for a good long hug and kiss before it's time to say good night.

All my love,

Tom

In the midst of all the turmoil, fighting, frantic to-and-fro movements of ships and men, and Tom's valiant efforts to keep Genevieve close by any means possible, Tom was still a chaplain, with all that title implies. Throughout his life and career, Tom was devoted to his service to God and man. Aboard ship he was truly the pastor for his flock, conducting regular Sunday morning worship services, even while underway at sea (fig. 3-15), and officiating at events such as shown in figure 3-16, where he is conducting prayers over the flag-draped coffin of a fallen comrade. In addition, he was spiritual counselor and leader, confidential advisor, writer-of-letters for crewmen, chief librarian, educator and lecturer, chief tour guide for groups of crewmen on shore liberty (fig. 3-17), ombudsman, and simply a good friend to all. In short, the Navy life kept him busily engaged during every waking hour.

The Young Men's Christian Association remained an important part of Tom's life, even while in the Navy. The YMCA was active in Asia during the twenties and had a large presence in Chefoo. The executive secretary of the

Navy Y in Chefoo was Paul W. Brown, and the two men formed a lifelong bond of friendship and mutual support. When his ship was in port, Tom often conducted Sunday services in the large meeting hall at the Chefoo YMCA (fig. 3-18).

Amusingly enough, Tom wasn't above employing a bit of a stratagem in the service of preaching the gospel. Normally, crewmen who were due Sunday shore liberty were required to stay aboard ship until the afternoon. However, Tom rather cleverly talked Four-star Admiral Clarence S. Williams into issuing an order granting extended liberty to all men who took the early morning shore boat to attend church at the Y. Once the 9:00 a.m. service was over, the men were free to stay ashore until the evening boat came to return them to the ship. Needless to say, the chaplain found the effect on church attendance to be most agreeable.

As he had during his earlier days in Persia in 1911–14, he took thousands of pictures of people, places, and events in Chefoo (fig. 3-19). His images of the cultural and religious sites in China form a fascinating pictorial record of the times. On many occasions, Tom conducted groups of crewmen on tours of what he termed the "more worthwhile" places ashore. He felt great concern about the less savory establishments in port cities attracting particularly the young men of the Navy, especially after payday. He wrote to Genevieve about his tour guide activities.

2/12/27

Dearest:

… Took about twenty-five men on a trip to the little temple on Honan Road and up to the Bankers Guild House. Both beautiful, both are temples to the god of wealth. Now to bed.

Love, love, love.

Your own,

Tommy

The ships of the Asiatic Fleet periodically returned to Cavite, where they took part in gunnery exercises, took on provisions, and underwent needed repairs and maintenance. Tom and Genevieve eagerly looked forward to such reunions. However, as the following letter from Tom demonstrates, the demands of the Navy took precedence over any private plans.

Sunday Night, bowling along northward

Dearest:

It is late, and I'm tired, but I must have my chat with you before I turn in. The ship was under way when I woke up this morning.... Church was rigged in the same place as last Sunday.... We were taking on stores from lighters until one o'clock.... I preached on "Making Good on the Asiatic." ... Got ready for circulation some forty or fifty books on China and Chinese affairs. After that, prepared an informal talk on China.... The compartment was jammed, must have been one hundred and fifty, and they seemed interested....

We have no news from Shanghai, and no one is making any plans for his family until we get there and find out what conditions may be. Hotels are probably crowded, with people leaving Hankow. I hated to leave you last night; it was so unexpected and broke into our plans so badly. I hope that you won't be too lonely, and that conditions will be such that you can come on up here before long, if we remain. Mrs. Williams is to go to Baguio tomorrow, so the Admiral told me. I guess he likes this as little as any of us. But what can't be cured must be endured, so here's love to you via telepathy as I write and by mail steamer ten days later. Heaps of love, and then some more.

Your own,

Tom

Admiral Williams was the senior officer over all of the eight-nation forces gathered and ready for action in China at the time. Even the admiral's wife had to endure the same separations the other Navy wives did. Tom's reference to books on China and to his informal talk make it clear that one of the duties he undertook aboard ship was to help the crew understand why they were in Asiatic waters. Later in the same hurried trip to Shanghai, he wrote a letter expressing his deep desire to be with Genevieve, but also the very real concerns of all for the safety of loved ones.

Wednesday Night, not far from the Fairway Buoy, off Woosung

Dearest Genevieve:

How does it sound in a letter to be called Genevieve? Not quite so well as though it were actually being whispered in your ear, I know, though sometimes when I'm sitting down in the quiet of my stateroom I seem to feel you very near. Do you have these same experiences? I hope so, for they are very dear moments. Of course, they show that I miss you, and I'm going to miss you more when we get to Shanghai. I'm afraid it isn't going to be wise for you to come up here in the near future, however, for if trouble does come, and evacuation becomes necessary, we shall want as few additional ones to look after as possible. We have already been figuring how many we could accommodate on the ship, if necessary, and so have the other ships. Plans are being made for any contingency, so far as the future can be prepared for today.... So this is going to be the goodnight sentence, with a heap of lovin' thrown in, via letter, and perhaps, for you seem near me this evening, via telepathy. So, nighty-night.

Your loving hubby,

Tom

After the ship had arrived in Shanghai, Tom wrote again expressing his longing for Genevieve to be with him, but with more details about the precarious situation preventing it. At that time foreigners in the interior were in mortal danger from marauding bands of armed revolutionaries who blamed the "foreign devils" for all their woes. Even missionaries were not spared. This stimulated the powers to send armed rescue parties to escort people to Shanghai, and to mass troops and ships there in order to establish that city as what they referred to as "Fortress Shanghai." Tom wrote about going ashore in Shanghai:

1/18

Dearest:

I've been mighty lonely for you today.... It was time for tea, and how I wish I might have walked down to the Astor and found you there. Had a lovely afternoon with a fire in the grate, making it cheerful and warm in spite of the chilly atmosphere outside. But that's enough, you'll be getting lonely too, and that won't do. For I'm very much afraid that it's going to be some little time before you should come up here. Yesterday I went over to the Missions Building to look up Ralph Wells.... Had quite a chat with Dr. Lowrie, who went through the Boxer trouble, and he fears that we may have something of the same kind of thing soon. That is the fear of all who have responsibility for missionaries up country, and Wells told me that our Board is following the lead of the British and have already ordered all our people from Hunan to come out, and may order others soon.... Talked with the captain of the Ysabel *and he feels more is to come right after Chinese New Years, two weeks away. So, you may be sure that none of us want our wives to come into such a possible situation needlessly.*

Now, if only you were here to tuck me in and kiss me goodnight, I'd have turned in an hour ago. I'm not feeling one hundred percent tonight, for the steam heat and sharp weather when I step outside have given me a bit of a sore throat and catarrhal condition, which is very annoying. So it goes, we are too hot one place and too cold the next, so why worry? I must to bed, so nighty-night with love and kisses, and all the sentimental rest with which true lovers always close their letters.

Your own hubby,

Tommy

The "Boxer trouble" Tom refers to was an armed uprising that had taken place at the turn of the century, commonly called the Boxer Rebellion. The term boxer had been coined by the westerners then in China to describe the martial arts practitioners who made up the ranks of the revolutionaries. To westerners, any form of martial activity appeared like western-style boxing, hence the name. The boxers, to whom their martial art took on semi-religious meaning, were devoted to cleansing China of what they felt was the polluting influence of westerners, particularly missionaries. Indeed, a number of missionaries lost their lives. The Boxer Rebellion had eventually been put down when the British sent twenty thousand troops to Peking where the West had gathered their citizens in a defensible compound and had been holding off a siege by boxers.

A short while later, Tom wrote, recognizing how hard it was for Genevieve to be constantly left alone while he sailed away to possible war.

1/20

Well, Old Honey Bunch:

Isn't that a dignified beginning? Maybe you think I ought to be more sedate when I write, but I like to call you pet names through the mail as well as when I am with you, so that's that.... Manila might have a good many refugees if it comes to real trouble up here, for already the Pillsbury *has started from Foochow with thirty from there, after our mission was looted.... No one knows whether the situation we are sitting on is loaded or not, and we probably won't find out until after Chinese New Year. Meanwhile, we are standing by for trouble, and not sending for our families. This letter won't reach you as quickly as the last one did, for this one won't catch a destroyer as did the last one. I've met a number of the men from the* Huron *ashore, men who have gone to the* Asheville *and* Sacramento, *especially Marines.*

I hope you are finding something to do which makes the time pass quickly and happily. It is always hard to be the one left behind, I know,

Dearest. Yet that's the way it goes so often, the man fares forth to fight while the woman stays at home to keep the fires burning. But when you're in the tropics and don't need the fires, it is doubly hard, isn't it? So I send a double amount of love, though I've been sending it all each time.

Ever your faithful husband,

Tom

Genevieve wrote Tom letters during this period, addressed c/o USS *Pittsburgh*, Shanghai.

2/7

Dearest Tommy:

Letters are coming most every day. How nice it is to receive them. The one you sent by the destroyers came today, postmarked USS Peary. *The checks came all right. Before I deposited them there was a balance of $135.06.... I am still undecided about taking passage on the* Empress of Canada. *I don't want to stay here after March. Do you think we could stay at the Y?*

2/8

Dearest Tommy:

Another day gone and you are no nearer. The Woods change their plans so often that I am just going ahead with my plans and not try to make them fit in with theirs. Chaplain Wood said yesterday they had received word that unless they were sent up to Shanghai because of trouble, the Black Hawk *would be here until April 18, and that Lenore and the children would go to Baguio after her operation to stay until they leave for China.*

(NOTE: The USS *Black Hawk* was a destroyer tender supporting Destroyer Squadron Five of the Asiatic Fleet.)

Mr. and Mrs. Barnes are going home on the President Taft, also Mrs. Barnes' mother, Mrs. Croft. So look them up while the Taft is in Shanghai, as I'll probably give them a box of candy—fudge—for you.

... I get mighty lonesome for you, old honey, especially when I look up and see the moon shining brightly. I'll be coming up soon, if you don't watch out. All my love goes to you in this envelope.

Nighty night,

Genevieve

On March 24, 1927, ships of the United States, Britain, and Japan traveled up the Yangtze River to Nanking on an urgent rescue mission. Foreigners, including Americans, had been attacked in a well-organized assault by Chinese troops and forced to seek shelter in the consulate on Socony Hill, where they were under siege. The American commander of the flotilla, Lt. Commander Roy C. Smith, Jr., was under orders to avoid direct armed conflict with troops of a nation with which we were officially at peace. However, fearing an imminent massacre, and in violation of his orders, he prepared to lay a barrage down around the refuge in order to discourage the Chinese troops from moving in and committing the massacre. Then, in further violation of his orders, he sent a shore party to fight their way to the consulate and escort the refugees back to the waiting ships. He was reported to have told the officer in charge of the barrage, "Well, I'll either get a medal or a court martial out of this, but let her go, Benny!" The ships, loaded with refugees, then returned to Shanghai, running a gauntlet of armed and threatening Chinese troops lining the river banks.

It was during this same period that the fateful event, referred to earlier as the Tragedy of the Revolution, took place. On April 12, 1927, Chiang Kai-Shek's forces committed the stealthy round up and brutal execution of thousands of followers of Chen Duxiu in Shanghai. This event was known as "The Purging of the Party" by the perpetrators and "The Shanghai Massacre" by those on the losing side. Bitter-armed struggle became the rule in China thereafter, with Chiang's forces gaining the upper hand for a time. Mao was forced into the countryside, where he continued the struggle with a ragtag army of peasants.

That same month personal tragedy struck Tom when he received news that his father, Newton Jasper Kirkpatrick, had passed away. The elder Kirkpatrick had been at various times a carpenter, a schoolteacher, and a minister, and he was a powerful role model for his son. Tom wrote the following remarkable letter to his bereaved mother, amply demonstrating both his devotion to her, as well as his ability to put aside his own hurt and act almost as her spiritual counselor and comforter.

At home, after church, April 22, (1927)

Dearest Mother,

There is no need to tell you that all of us children will be thinking of you with especial tenderness and love next Thursday. For we know that the entrance into the Heavenly Home means a temporary parting with loved ones here below, which cannot but be sad, though the gleam of Heaven's eternal sunshine bursts through the clouds of loneliness. I wish that all of us might be with you, so that the loneliness might be lessened by our presence, but since this cannot be, we shall be holding you up in arms of prayer, that our Heavenly Father may grant you some special blessing of comfort. I am sure that father would ask nothing better, than that each of us should be engaged in honoring our Heavenly Father as we serve him in the service of our fellowmen in our various places of duty and lines of endeavor, and that as a family our circle is still unbroken in the light of the Salvation He has wrought for us. Genevieve and I join in love to you Dearest Mother.

Your son,

Roy

Tom was still in China when on September 7, 1927, Mao's peasant army staged a revolt known as the Autumn Harvest Uprising in long-contested Hunan Province and Jangxi Province. It allowed Mao to establish a short-lived government called the Hunan Soviet. However, the KMT forces and the landlords of Hunan ultimately prevailed, forcing Mao to retreat into a rugged area known as the Jinggang Mountains, on the border between Hunan and Jiangxi province. Mao went on to develop a new strategy, rural in nature, depending primarily on guerrilla tactics rather than pitched battles between two armies.

It is unclear from the correspondence between Tom and Genevieve whether she ever made it back to the Chinese mainland for any significant period of time before Tom's tour of duty with the Asiatic Fleet ended. In the fall of 1927, Tom received orders that relieved him of his fleet chaplain duties and brought him back stateside. They were relieved to leave China and return home to the safety of California.

On August 26, 1927, Tom was detached from the USS *Pittsburgh* and ordered to report for duty at the Naval Training Center, San Diego. Tom became the base chaplain on October 24, 1927, and he and Genevieve began a new phase of their life together. At last, they were able to settle down for a time with each other in their own stateside home. His tour in San Diego lasted two years, before he was once again ordered to sea duty.

Fig. 3-1 Nationalist Revolutionary Army enters Wuhan

Fig. 3-2 Tom and Genevieve enjoy rickshaw ride in Chefoo

Fig. 3-3 Tom and Genevieve enjoy each other

Fig. 3-4 Beach Picnic, Chefoo Tom and Genevieve really must enjoy the food

Fig. 3-5 Manila home

Fig. 3-6 Playful moment in Hong Kong

Fig. 3-7 U.S.S. Pittsburgh New flagship of the Asiatic Fleet replaced Huron

Fig. 3-8 Armed sailors aboard U.S.S. Huron

Fig. 3-9 Marine contingent aboard U.S.S. Pittsburgh

Fig. 3-10 U.S.S. Asheville Tom had friends aboard ill-fated gunboat, sunk in WW-II.

Fig. 3-11 Gunboat U.S.S. Sacramento Was in Pearl Harbor on December 7th and was credited with shooting down two attacking aircraft.

Fig. 3-12 U.S.S. Parrott Took part in torpedo attack in Balikpapan Bay in 1942, then served in Atlantic for rest of war on escort service.

Fig. 3-13 U.S.S. Peary Sunk while defending Darwin, Australia, guns blazing against air raid attack in 1942, with the loss of 100 hands.

Fig. 3-14 U.S.S. McCormick Served on convoy escort duty in the Atlantic in WW-II.

Fig. 3-15 Church Call Aboard Ship

Fig. 3-16 Leading prayers over the coffin of a fallen comrade in Chefoo.

Fig. 3-17 Chaplain leading tour for Huron sailors in Chefoo

Fig. 3-18 Tom conducting services at Chefoo YMCA

3-19 Temple interior One example of the many photos Tom took while in Asia.

CHAPTER 4

Home Again: San Diego Naval Training Center

For many years, San Diego has been the headquarters of the Navy's Eleventh Naval District. At one point, it was home to fully one-sixth of the entire U.S. Navy's fleet. The city and surrounding areas became home to more than a dozen important military installations, including such behemoths as the Marine Corps' Camp Pendleton in the northern part of the county, the Marine Corps Recruit Depot, Miramar Naval Air Station, North Island Naval Air Station, and many others. The Naval Training Center's role in this vast military presence was to serve as the primary place where raw recruits became seamen.

Tom's new assignment at the Naval Training Center (NTC) saw him reporting for duty at a base only four years old. Prior to 1920, the city fathers of San Diego, wishing to improve the city's economy, had offered the government two hundred acres of prime land adjacent to San Diego Bay. They lobbied for the Navy to relocate the Recruit Training Station from San Francisco to San Diego. In 1919, due to the efforts of Congressman William Kettner, Congress took the bait and authorized the plan. Construction began in 1921, and the brand new base was commissioned in 1923.

Over time, the base grew substantially, eventually reaching 550 acres in size. During World War II the base was home to 33,000 men, and during the Korean War, it housed 40,000 men. However, in 1927, when Tom reported for duty, it was a relatively small base, still under construction. The surrounding San Diego suburb of Loma Portal was still far from built out, consisting of sizable areas largely devoted to sage brush, barrel cactus, jackrabbits, snakes, tarantulas, coyotes, and foxes.

The Naval Training Center remained a prime facility for providing basic training to new recruits until the Base Realignment and Closure Act of 1993 at the end of the Cold War. NTC was officially closed in 1997, with the land and buildings being turned over to the city. It is now a civilian-occupied development called Liberty Station.

In the early days, there were two areas within NTC. At the southern end there was a "detention" area, known as Camp Ingram, where brand new recruits lived while they were subjected to intense physical conditioning and schooling in the traditions and basics of life in the Navy and especially shipboard protocol. After up to eight weeks of this *really* basic training, they were allowed to move to "Main Unit" at the northern end of the base. There, they completed enough higher-level training that they were deemed fit for duty with the fleet, though many went on to more advanced training in various specialties before deployment.

Tom and Genevieve moved into rented temporary quarters not far from NTC, while Tom established himself in his new role as base chaplain. His duties there were in many ways similar to those on board ship. He preached the gospel on Sundays to the men at the base, oversaw the multi-faith use of the base chapel, acted as counselor and ombudsman, established a small lending library on the base, edited the weekly base newspaper, *The Hoist*, and generally looked after the welfare and morale of the young men undergoing basic training. He and Genevieve began their effort to finally start a family.

Since they had a short-term lease, they began to look around for a larger home, assuming they would be in San Diego for awhile. During this period, Genevieve took a rail trip to the Midwest and East Coast to visit family and friends she had not seen for several years. This time, Tom was the one left behind. While he continued searching for a home, he wrote letters to Genevieve, addressed to arrive before she did at the various stops along her route. Clearly he missed her very much.

10/20

Dearest:

I surely wish you were here to help decide the house question, for you spend more time than I do in the home.... It sure is good to know definitely the date that you'll be home again, even though it is the last day but one that the ticket will allow. Naughty Mamma! ... I'm still as lonesome as ever, old Dear. Time doesn't seem to make much difference, for it's as bad now as it was five weeks ago, when you had just left. That's a long time to desert a hard-working husband, isn't it? As a matter of fact, he can't seem to get down to work as hard as when you're home. So you'd better come on back before all my old sermons run out. May have to use one tomorrow, for I haven't prepared one, though vague ideas have been coming and going. It's a dreadful state for a minister to be in. Give my love to all the family, and tell Mary Ann and Mame that I'm going to write soon. Tell them if we take the Hallinan house there will be room for all the family next summer. With worlds of love to you, Sweetheart, and eagerly awaiting the thirtieth, when you'll be back in my arms once more. Love and kisses,

*even though we've been married five whole years.
Then some more, just for good measure.*

Your own hubby,

Tom

10/21

Dearest,

*Here it is, half past five, Sunday afternoon. It is
almost dark, and the lights are on. I've been
lying at ease on the davenport with a blaze in
the fireplace listening to a very good program
from KFI, a Biblical drama,* The Third Soldier,
*and then the half hour of music by the two
sisters who sing the old-time songs and hymns.
Sort of soothing, and yet it makes me pensive
and more lonesome for you. We've enjoyed this
fireplace, haven't we? And we must find a house
with another. And also, some additional means
of heat. After dinner at the Churchill today, I
cruised about Mission Hills a bit, saw several
houses that looked fair from the outside.... Am
almost to the point of asking to keep this place
until December 1 so we can house hunt together.
Does that sound good or bad to you?*

...Nine more days, Darling! They're going to drag!

Heaps of love,

Tom

Tom's reference to the need for additional means of
heat no doubt stems from the fact that homes in
Southern California were commonly built without
furnaces in those days. At most, there might have been a
few tiny wall-mounted gas or electric burners. Years later

many homes were retrofitted with honest-to-goodness forced air heating, much to the relief of the occupants.

Tom and Genevieve were trying to start their family during this time, but had met with only disappointment. She suffered a total of three miscarriages before little Tommy was finally born in 1932. Tom wrote this letter to Genevieve expressing his heartfelt desire for a child.

10/23

Dearest:

This morning I woke up at about half past four with a wonderful dream just vanishing from my mind—I was getting our baby ready to take out in the car! It was a very real dream, and happy. Can it be an omen of what is to come to pass in the not too distant future? Would that it might be!

... I'm writing this using the card table in front of the fireplace in which a blaze is going merrily. Don't you wish you could be here with me to enjoy it all? I do. Of course, KFI is on the air also. I'm hoping you'll get my last Washington letter today or tomorrow, addressed in Rube's care, at the club. Also that the one mailed to you at St. Louis yesterday will be awaiting you. If so, you'll know I love you, and am counting the days until you return. God bless and keep you, Darling.

A heart full of love, from your own,

Tom

In spite of San Diego's heavy reliance on the Navy and the revenue it generated, relations between the Navy and the city's residents were not always cordial. In spite of its natural beauty and wonderful climate, many seamen have distinctly unpleasant memories of their time in San Diego. In fact, some men referred to the city derisively as "Dago." This inspired Tom to greater efforts to make the Navy a "good neighbor" to the city. There is reason to appreciate the negative attitudes of many in the city, particularly small businesses. They knew the transient nature of most seamen's residence in San Diego. Hence they frequently refused credit or service to Naval personnel for fear they would move to other duty stations far away and be unreachable for the collection of debts.

Tom made a real effort to build ties with influential people of San Diego. Even though he was a Navy chaplain, he also was, by his own statements, acting much as a civilian church minister would. The following letter illustrates his active involvement in the community at large. It also makes clear how much he missed Genevieve and found himself rattling about the house without her company.

Friday Night, September 21

Genevieve dear:

A week now, lacking a few hours, since you started on your trip, and it has been a long week. So long as I'm at the office or downtown I don't get so lonesome, but it is hard to spend the evening here at the house, even with the radio going full blast. I turn it on when I come in and keep it going until I'm ready for bed.

Have had a busy day today, working on my sermon until ten o'clock here and home, then a conference with twelve men at the office, a very pleasant luncheon at the Navy YMCA (monthly Board meeting, and it's an uplift to sit with that board, the big men of the city, and fine Christian men). After a bit of work at the office, I had to get back downtown for a meeting of the Community

Chest workers, and didn't get away from that until about half past five, so stayed down and had dinner at the Mission Cafeteria. Then smoked my cigar and read the evening paper in the lobby of the Grant, and came on out home about seven. Couldn't get down to work immediately, so sat and read Death Comes for the Archbishop *until just now, half past eight. That's a most interesting book, isn't it?*

Yesterday I didn't write, but was happy to get a whole bunch of postcards, as well as your night letter. I thought the family would be pleased with Mary Ann's increased weight, however she might feel about it. Tell her I'm writing Sunday.

A notice was left at the house yesterday, asking the names of those who would receive mail here, and stating that carrier service would begin on October 1. I have had a 5x7 enlargement made of mother in the rocking chair, and it is very good. What do you think of having some made and framed to send to the other children for Christmas?

Mrs. Green was here today, and did about three dollars worth of laundry, if sent to the laundry, as well as the cleaning. So I guess it is just as well to have her come. I put in one of those large tablecloths, but haven't examined to see how well she did it. Mr. Lalever was here Tuesday, and caught that gopher that was digging in by the dahlias. At least the gopher was caught in the trap, which he dragged back into the burrow so far it couldn't be located. Probably died somewhere in the burrow.

When I was downtown today I purchased a set of new spark plugs, and find a good deal more power now. One of the old ones was badly cracked, which probably accounts for the poor pulling on Torrey Pines that one night. Too bad you can't be on hand next Tuesday to see the opening of our new tennis court by the officers' quarters. The opening set is going to be thrilling, Captain Cole and Comdr. Abbett against Dr. Mears and myself. We'll have to have the station photographer on hand and run a picture in The Hoist. *So maybe you'll see it after all (fig. 4-1).*

Mrs. Mansfield called up a few minutes ago to ask if I was ready for another picnic. I suggested putting it off until one week from Monday, as Chaplains Dyer and Truitt are both away at the Methodist Episcopal Conference until Saturday night.

By the way, did I tell you that I saw another old Asiatic friend at the hospital who asked to be remembered to you! A hospital corpsman by the name of Willgrubey, a TSL man from one of the destroyers. You'd remember him by face if not by name.

Well, I must get to work on the sermon if it's to be done, one on "Damn the torpedoes, full speed ahead," in other words, on prayer, though it may not sound like it.

So, lots of love and kisses—I hate to go to bed these nights,

Tom

Tom refers to an old Asiatic friend in the hospital, which is the Balboa Naval Hospital in San Diego. Just as he visited crewmembers in sick bay on ship, he also visited men in the hospital while on shore duty.

Throughout his Navy career, he tried to connect with all the men aboard his ship or duty station, regardless of their rank or rating. Indeed, some of the seamen who had been transferred to other ships wrote him letters of thanks for his friendship and support while they had served together. Tom believed that one of the important duties of a Navy chaplain was to build relationships.

A few days later, Tom wrote a long letter to Genevieve with news of happenings at the base. He chafed a bit over the actions of the commanding officer who frustrated his efforts to set up the lending library on base in quarters he deemed most appropriate. As the base chaplain, he was also in charge of soliciting donations for the Community Chest, which was a fundraising organization for community projects. He was similarly displeased with the lack of interest expressed by the commanding officer in this endeavor. But, being a loyal officer, he accepted the situation and carried on. Meanwhile he continued his search for a home and reported his findings to Genevieve. The following letter reveals his frustrations, disappointments, and general "having a bad day" frame of mind.

10/26

Sweetheart,

This was to have been written last night but after I had a bite to eat, I sat down to listen to the radio for a minute and went to sleep. That shows the state I was in, so I tumbled into bed a bit before ten, though I didn't drop asleep immediately as I had expected. Saturday night I lay awake again, or couldn't go to sleep. Until about two o'clock. Don't know why, as I hadn't had any coffee since morning and had played golf, which usually gives me a good physical tiredness that makes me sleepy. So that's the reason this wasn't written last night. Yesterday was a rather unsatisfactory day, my sermon plan didn't develop, and I used two old ones, "Clear Ship for Action" in Camp Ingram and "The Greatest Game" for Main Unit. Had a whale of a crowd in Main Unit, for there was no liberty for recruits, who were held on board so as to march in a body to the rooting section at the game against the USS California. So there were close to six hundred at that service. Communion followed, with an unusually large crowd remaining— eighty. But no baptisms. The company that I had expected some from were on mess cook duty, which may account partly for that. But a day when I have to remind others of the religious right of way, to keep from having the whole day an uproar on account of football routine, is always rather unsatisfactory.

The worst thing that happened last week however was the receipt of a memo asking what changes would be necessary before moving the library to the checker hall. I thought I had put up enough discouragements to keep that idea from maturing in the captain's mind, but I was mistaken, for he has meanwhile had an estimate made (without conference with me) as to cost of changes, and obtained a small sum from the Bureau and issued the order for the shift. It is going to be very difficult to get what we need to make that space into a good library, but of course all we can do is to take what the captain decrees.

Saturday I stopped by a place in La Jolla, overlooking the sea beyond the Casa Manana, in fact, directly behind the hospital. The folks are anxious to rent it, and I promised to drop by today and measure the rooms. They claim it is very warm, *though the living room exposure is to the west. Am a bit afraid that the rooms are a trifle small for our furniture, but will know more about this later. Rather imagine that they will make me an offer on it of $65 per month, though they said they got $150 for it furnished during the summer. I intend to look around out there this afternoon, instead of playing golf, so you see how it goes. I hate to rent a place until you see it, and won't sign a lease until you've had a chance to see how you like it. I called up Miss Spinney's phone (office) just now and learned that she is no longer here. Am also going to scout around in the Workmans' vicinity.*

Well, old dear, I must get over to the office and make a report to Comdr. Kays regarding Community Chest. At 11:30 I talk to the main unit regarding same, and the company commanders then get the contribution. The campaign isn't going well, too little interest at the top. The only man who can get contributions from the officers is the commanding officer, by getting them together and showing a bit of personal interest, which he frankly says he doesn't have.

Heaps of love,

Tom

Tom was trying to build a base library and was frustrated over his commandant's arbitrary decision as to where to locate it. There is no record of the library other than a picture of Tom with his "Library Force" (fig. 4-2) standing in front of the building that Tom considered inadequate. However, the library was much better equipped in the 1940s, so later commandants apparently were considerably more receptive than Tom's superiors had been.

Tom took his involvement with the San Diego Community Chest seriously, and was frustrated over the general lack of support he got from above. He believed the organization provided a positive and needed contribution to life in San Diego. Genevieve believed in the organization as well. After she and Tommy moved back to San Diego in the later stages of World War II, she volunteered for and eventually became the president of the Big Sister League of San Diego. This was a service organization supported by the United Way, the successor to the Community Chest. It was not uncommon for Navy wives and their children to arrive in San Diego, trying to follow their husbands, only to find themselves stranded without resources or a place to sleep, their husbands having already been shipped out. The League operated a shelter to temporarily help these women avoid sleeping on the streets, and then assisted them to find long-term solutions.

Once Genevieve returned from her family trip, the couple renewed their search for permanent housing. Eventually they found a house in Loma Portal that had been previously rented by old Asiatic friends, Paul and Mabel Brown. Tom and Genevieve moved into their new home at 3045 James Street (fig. 4-3), only one block away from NTC. After settling in, the couple began entertaining men from NTC as part of Tom's base chaplain responsibilities.

Genevieve became a gracious hostess, as they invited their guests regularly for Sunday afternoon dinner (fig. 4-4). In addition, they socialized regularly with fellow officers and their spouses. In figure 4-5 Tom and Genevieve are hosting an informal afternoon tea attended by his tennis foursome plus others.

Tom kept working to gain support for the Community Chest. As editor of *The Hoist*, he ran an article in the November 26, 1927, issue about the lack of support for the organization. The chaplain encouraged base personnel to make a donation to "this worthy cause." The total donated was less than $150, much less than the previous year. The following year, Tom pulled out all of the stops. In addition to his previous efforts, he might have made a casual comment during a friendly round of golf with the admiral, to salutary effect. In any event, the Eleventh Naval District Commandant, Admiral Robertson, singled the Center out for praise in *The Hoist* on December 1, 1928, saying they had made the second best gain over the previous year of any unit in his command by tripling their donations.

The November 26, 1927, issue of *The Hoist* also included an article describing the very ship Tom was to serve aboard later.

NEW PLANE SHIP EYES OF NAVY

Aircraft Carrier Speediest Warship in Service; To Take the Langley's Place

On Wednesday Admiral Lattimer signed a chit for the receipt of "one aircraft carrier, Saratoga," from the American Brown-Boveri Electric Corporation, marking the beginning of the realization of the Navy's aerial building program. The Saratoga is the only first-class aircraft carrier in the Navy at present, for with her arrival the Langley will be used for its originally intended purpose, experimental research.

Speediest Afloat

The new ship is faster than any other large ship in the Navy, being capable of about thirty-five knots. She is electrically propelled by a plant of 180,000 horsepower similar in design to that aboard the Tennessee. Her flying deck is 880 feet long and 100 feet wide, about two acres of unbroken flying field; her stacks are on the side, rather than on the center line. She is equipped with a retarder to stop planes within 130 feet. Although almost all of the flying will be directly on and off the flying deck, she is also equipped with catapults for launching, and cranes for hoisting aboard seaplanes. Her armament consists of torpedo tubes, eight-inch guns, and five-inch semi-automatic anti-aircraft guns of the type aboard the newer battleships. With this armament she will not be entirely defenseless against aerial bombing attack. She will be manned by 2,200 men, including aviation personnel for all her planes. Her radio equipment is necessarily more elaborate than that of other ships, since she must be able to communicate with different planes in the air besides the regular ship's traffic. She will carry about 85 planes, Boeing fighters, Martin bombers, and Vought Corsair observation planes. To Join Battle Fleet the Saratoga *was received by Admiral Latimer and turned over to Captain H. E. Yarnell, who is in command. She will be manned and supplied soon, after which she will take a shakedown cruise to parts as yet unknown. After this cruise she will join the battle fleet.*

The *Langley* was the very first ship in the American Navy to have a true flight deck where planes could take off. Other ships, such as the battleships, had been fitted with a catapult capable of launching a floatplane. The floatplane's mission was to conduct long-range surveillance, then land in the water and be hoisted aboard by crane, to be remounted on the catapult. *Langley* was also the first ship in the Navy powered by electric motors. This gave her a speed capability of 15 knots, far below that of the aircraft carriers that were to follow. The new propulsion technology worked well enough that the Navy decided to use it in the much larger, much faster second-generation carriers *Lexington* and *Saratoga*. *Langley* had originally been commissioned as the USS *Jupiter*, a collier (a ship designed to refuel the older coal-burning ships of the fleet). The *Langley* had been converted (fig. 4-6) in 1920 for use in studying the effectiveness of air power and in developing tactics and techniques for its use at sea. During this period, the Navy was engaged in converting from coal power to oil power, hence the need for a collier was disappearing. *Jupiter's* superstructure was removed, her stacks were diverted to stick out at her port side and be capable of pivoting down below flight deck level, and an 800-foot flat flight deck was added. She was given the designation CV-1. In contrast, the USS *Saratoga*, along with her sister ship, USS *Lexington*, were the first two ships built from the keel up specifically for the purpose of handling aircraft. *Lexington* was given the designation CV-2 and *Saratoga* CV-3 (fig. 4-7).

The *Langley* was converted to a seaplane tender in the late 1930s. In this configuration, she continued in service until Japanese bombs struck her on February 27, 1942 (fig. 4-8), costing sixteen lives and disabling her, forcing her scuttling. The *Saratoga* served during World War II with distinction, sustaining heavy damage from Japanese aerial attacks. The comment in *The Hoist* concerning the ship's armament making her "not entirely defenseless against aerial bombing attack" proved wrong. Her eight-inch and five-inch turret-mounted guns can be seen clearly from the side in figure 4-9, a configuration inherited from the era of the battleship. When they were later discovered to be nearly useless for air defense, they were replaced and augmented with guns specifically designed for the purpose.

When Tom published the article about *Saratoga*, he had no way of knowing that this technologically advanced ship was to be his next posting, or that he was destined to participate aboard her in war games, known as "fleet problems," where naval forces engaged in mock battles. These exercises proved crucial in preparing the Navy for World War II.

Fig. 4-1 Inaugurating the new tennis court

Fig. 4-2 Tom's "Library Force" In front of the building he thought inadequate.

Fig. 4-3 3045 James St. Tom and Genevieve's home while he was at NTC.

Fig. 4-4 Sailors from NTC attending Sunday dinner with Tom and Genevieve

Fig. 4-5 Tom and Genevieve attending tea with other NTC officers and wives

Fig. 4-6 U.S.S. Langley Navy's first aircraft carrier, converted from a Collier.

Fig. 4-7 Saratoga being built

Fig. 4-8 Langley under attack   After conversion to Seaplane Tender in WW-II.

Fig. 4-9 CV-3 Saratoga   Battleship-era gun turrets visible. Later converted to AA guns.

CHAPTER 5

At Sea Once More, USS *Saratoga*

On July 5, 1930, Tom received orders detaching him from his duty as base chaplain in San Diego. And so he and Genevieve were about to endure another period of separation. Tom reported for duty on July 9, 1930, aboard the USS *Saratoga*. Genevieve was left behind to keep the home fires burning, living in a rented apartment in Long Beach, *Saratoga's* home port. Between sorties at sea, the ship spent brief periods in port, allowing Tom and Genevieve time together. Then the ship would once again be off to sea to participate in the latest fleet problems. Each year the Navy challenged *Saratoga* and the rest of the fleet with a new set of war games. *Saratoga* was particularly active, since she was the prototype and test bed for carrier design as well as the platform for developing the Naval Air Wing tactics the Navy would use in case of war.

    Saratoga, affectionately called *Sara* by her crew, was a busy ship throughout the 1930s. She ranged up and down the West Coast, the Panama Canal Zone, and the Hawaiian Islands. Periodically she traveled to the Bremerton Naval Shipyard on Puget Sound for needed repairs and modifications. All this time, she was developing naval air tactics and testing them in the fleet problems being thrown at her and the other ships in the fleet. In these games, *Saratoga* was usually one of the high priority targets for the opposing force, in recognition of her growing importance.

Tom served aboard *Saratoga* until May 1, 1932, before being detached to report to the Brooklyn Naval Shipyard. Not long before he left, *Saratoga* participated in the fleet problem for 1932, which took place in Hawaiian waters from January 31 to March 19. The following year *Saratoga* returned to Hawaiian waters again to take part in the fleet problem for 1933. On her return trip, she launched a successful mock air attack on the city of Long Beach, demonstrating how naval air power could be effective against targets on land. Later, *Saratoga* participated in Fleet Problem XIX in March of 1938 during which she launched a successful surprise air "attack" on Pearl Harbor from a point one hundred miles offshore, an eerie foreshadowing of Japan's devastating surprise attack on Pearl Harbor on December 7, 1941. Due in large measure to *Saratoga's* efforts, the era of naval air power superiority was beginning, just as the era of the battleship was declining.

In an interesting historical footnote, around the time Tom was leaving NTC and reporting aboard *Saratoga*, he sent a copy of a sermon titled "That Question of Prayer" to the famous explorer Admiral Richard E. Byrd. In the sermon, he talked about Admiral Byrd's Antarctic expedition, when he had flown over the South Pole. Admiral Byrd replied to Tom, and his letter is shown in figure 5-1.

Soon after reporting aboard *Saratoga*, Tom sent Genevieve a letter, written on stationery from his hotel room at the Lafayette Hotel in Long Beach.

Dearest,

How do you like the paper? You always carry off some small bars of soap, but I specialize in writing paper. Somehow it seems more like a letter to someone away when the paper is from a hotel.

I hardly realized you had gone until I started back from Los Angeles alone last night and put the car in the Breakers Hotel garage. It turned out that I took Gladys to dinner, for Will had a board meeting, and Helen said she had burned the potatoes and didn't have much else. So we two went to the French place we've heard about, Taix's Café, down in that railway section. Tables covered with spotless linoleum, in imitation of marble. Six people at a table. A big tureen of delicious soup was brought, and we helped ourselves. Good French bread in abundance, but no butter. When we had finished the soup, a platter of sliced ox tongue, with a delicious cream sauce came on, with another large dish of wonderful boiled potatoes. We passed these around and by the time these were finished, the waitress brought in a platter of sliced boiled beef, another of baked squash, and a huge bowl of crisp lettuce with French dressing on it. Then came some cheese, and a big dish of walnuts and apples. The signal that you wanted coffee was to finish your water, put your spoon in the glass, and wait for the coffee. At our table were two couples, one of the men Jewish (a musician now in Movietone) and the other apparently French (a salesman). Both men had lived in St. Louis, the latter down in Carondelet. Price of the meal, fifty cents. Tips not the rule. A good time was had by all. And maybe you think the place doesn't do a big business with as many limousines as Fords out in front. In fact, more.

Today has gone badly. Didn't sleep well, as usual, the first night on board. Went ashore to the annual Navy Relief Society meeting at the Navy YMCA and saw most of the chaplains and Mrs.

Leonard and Mrs. Dittmar. Went looking for some white canvas shoes over there, but came out with some badly needed golf shoes that were on sale at five dollars. Then I came on back to L.B. and found some white shoes at $3.96. Dropped down to say hello to the Kerrs before catching the 5:45 to the ship, but remained for dinner with them at the hotel. They moved into "415" today. She was mailing you the letter from Mrs. Jupp because she wasn't sure you had taken the address. They had a pleasant visit at San Diego. We had planned on a movie, but the doctor was tired, so we sat in the lobby, smoked, talked, heard Amos n' Andy, and said good-bye in time for me to catch the 9:15. I've finished unpacking the two suitcases since then, and have stayed up too late, for it is 11:10. I sent night letters to Charles and Mame. Hope you are having a good trip and that all goes smoothly at Chicago. Also that your trunk comes through promptly. Let Will know if it doesn't.

Lots of love and then some more. Your own,

Tommy

P.S. Hello, Everybody!

Tom may not have realized how prescient he was when he sent the following letter to Genevieve from the *Saratoga*. His observations about *Saratoga* being a "working ship" would resonate with today's carrier crews. The flight deck is in constant use launching and retrieving aircraft, and the crewman who is not constantly in a high state of alertness can easily suffer a serious accident. Figure 5-2 gives an idea of what the chaos on the flight deck might have looked like when the ship was underway and preparing to launch her aircraft.

2/11

From Saratoga *in Canal Zone (On stationery from Lafayette Hotel in Long Beach)*

Dearest:

Three days since my last scribble to you. Wonder how you are going to enjoy the task of deciphering these letters. Shall I use the typewriter? These three days have been busy ones for the ship. Flight operations each morning and endless shifting of planes about on the flight deck and in and out of the hangar deck during the afternoon and evening. I begin to realize how truly Askin spoke when he said this was a "working" ship. A battleship can't compare with it. But the men will have a rest these next four days, for we are due to anchor early tomorrow and not get underway until some time Sunday evening or night when the battle problem begins. I got out the ship's paper early, to carry information about Panama, so won't have that to keep me on board. I'll enclose one, as it tells about the problem that will engage our attention next week.

Tomorrow morning I'm expecting to have my first flight, across the Isthmus and back, with Ralph Wood in one of our ship's planes such as we used for the weekend trips to San Diego. It is a beautiful trip according to all reports. I'll write all about it later. By the way, do you remember the Schutt's mentioning that they had a relative in the Saratoga *squadron? I had a chat with him yesterday and find him a delightful chap. Most of these aviators are up-and-coming fellows, who make the ship and mess rooms very lively. The four-squadron commanders are at the "first ward" table. The rest are scattered about the ward room and J.O. mess as their class and signal number may entitle them. Tomorrow evening will probably see the mess quite depleted, as freedom to get ashore for relaxation will be appreciated after these strenuous days. And next week will be much worse, with both day and night flying.*

I've wondered how you found all the family and what you've been doing. You did nobly as a correspondent en route to Chicago. Hope you have a couple of letters en route right now. I'll enclose a letter from Mother that came at San Diego.

Hope you are enjoying your visit so much that you aren't missing your hubby as much as he misses you.

Heaps of love,

Your own Tommy

Tom's comments about the seating arrangements in the officer's ward room and the J.O. (junior officer) mess highlight how traditional and hierarchical the U.S. Navy was, patterned as it was after the much older Royal Navy of Great Britain.

While *Saratoga* was training in the Canal Zone, Tom had the opportunity to take his first ever airplane ride: a two-hour tour over the Canal Zone, taking off and landing on the *Saratoga's* flight deck in an open cockpit fighter aircraft, (fig. 5-3) an experience he described as leaving his ears ringing for two days, but not a word about the dangers involved in making carrier landings. Figure 5-4 shows the same type of aircraft doing a flyby of *Saratoga*.

2/12   (from Panama, at anchor)

Dearest:

Well, this is going to be short, and I hope sweet, for it should reach you not long after Valentine's Day, and you're my Valentine. This morning I had the thrill that comes but once in a lifetime, my first airplane ride. Also a privilege that few folks ever have of taking that first ride over the Panama Canal. Ralph Wood promised that he'd ride me across some day and last evening said that he'd leave early this morning. At 8:30 we took off and were in the air two hours. He was in command of the N.A.S. at Coco Solo for a time and knows this region thoroughly, so as we passed over the various points of interest, or were about to do so, he'd write me a note and pass it back to me. Thus we saw all the points of interest that can be seen from one ocean to the other. Went up to 4,000 feet to get a look at both oceans at the same time. Later we went up to 8,000 so as to get a look at the site of Porto Bello and Nombre de Dios, which Columbus saw in 1500. On our return trip, the Los Angeles appeared coming toward us, so we climbed a bit and then circled around her at a safe distance. So I guess I had all that one ride could possibly entitle a person to, unless it was a parachute jump, for which I have no hankering. Not me. My ears haven't stopped ringing yet, but that's a small price for a two-hour ride over the Canal.

I mailed you three letters in the regular mail, which should reach you in about ten days. This is supposed to catch tomorrow's airmail, and I must hurry, for I want to make the boat in ten minutes. Shall I take a look around, for you? Well, the boat is being called away, and it's too long a distance to risk missing it, so here's a pile of love and greetings to all the family. Three days of rest and

*recreation here for us, and then a week of real
work. All my love.*

Your hubby,

Tom

And real work it was to be aboard a carrier in the
tropics during simulated wartime. From the number of
different types of ships Tom describes, the Navy devoted
considerable resources to performing the fleet problems.
He doesn't make it sound like much fun, just hard,
miserable, sweaty work. However, it wasn't so all the
time. Occasionally the crew enjoyed some lighter
moments like the invasion of a Hollywood film crew to
stage a burial at sea. As the chaplain, Tom presided over
the mock funeral on camera, and if the scene made it
past the cutting room floor, he was in the movies. He
wrote Genevieve about the part he played in the film.

3/8   (at Bahia Honda, Panama Republic)

Dearest:

*I have just thirty minutes in which to get this
written and in the mail, for word passed a
moment ago that there would be mail leaving the
ship at 11:30. Haven't written since last Monday,
and in fact there has been little about which to
write. We've been going here and there off
Panama, engaged in various maneuvers in which
submarines were making attacks on the carriers
and battleships, and cruisers were attacking, and
so forth. Had two nights when we darkened ship,
which meant much heat until eleven o'clock. But it
hasn't been so hot as previously, until we dropped
anchor here yesterday morning. Since then,
mucho heat.*

Was delighted to get a letter from you yesterday, when a tug brought some mail for us from Panama. Your letter of February 21 it was. Hope that the birthday party was a big success and that neither of the honored guests feels so much older for having passed another milestone. As for that children's party at the Gooding home, tell Mame I am shocked at her. Tell her that costume was worse than her bathing suit and that I can't understand why she objected so much to putting on a modern cut after the costume at your party the other night. Tell her I'll expect her to blossom out in the latest style her next visit to California.

Incidentally, tell Nettie that she'd better visit us this next summer, for I've broken into the movies. Yes indeed, and a hot time it was. Yesterday morning following quarters, we shot the big scene in the picture that is being filmed by MGM with our cooperation. The hero of the picture, if you can call him that, is killed while saving the life of the pilot of the machine of which he is the mechanic, and yesterday we buried him at sea. As the officiating chaplain I had my part to do, so tell Nettie that she now has an uncle who has been in the movies. It was desperately hot on the flight deck during the time we were getting the scene taken, and the men lined up for the ceremony sweated until they were wet through. One electrician's mate keeled over, I'm told, but I didn't notice it. We were afraid that the crowd might not enter into the spirit of the occasion and might spoil the effect with their smiles, but I'm told that it was as solemn an occasion as a real funeral. The close-ups will be shot later at the studio probably, and I may go over for them. At least I told the director who's on board that I'd do so if I film properly and can get away for it. Naturally I'll be taking over a number of sightseeing parties from the ship shortly after we get back to Long Beach, for all the crowd are interested in seeing how the movies are made on the lot.

I just came down from church, where the crowd was disappointing for a Sunday at sea where there's no liberty. Guess the crowd just want to lie around in any corner they can find that is cool, and haven't energy enough to get up for church when church call sounds. Had about 175 there this morning, with 42 at communion. My reported numbers are smaller than Ackiss' were, though my yeoman swears that the congregations have been larger. But it is a steady group that attends; I see the same faces Sunday after Sunday. The series of sermons I'm preaching is not of the popular type, but I feel that they are giving those who attend something real.

Last night we had a smoker, and I was mighty glad when it was all over in a fairly successful way. Our men didn't come out well in the bouts we arranged with fighters from the Mississippi, but all in all it was quite a successful affair. I'm told that it was the first evening smoker ever held on the flight deck here, which perhaps accounts for the fact that I couldn't find anyone who knew just how to arrange for it. I learned a lot. And I'm more than ever convinced that the battleship chaplains don't know what real hard work is in such affairs. I can see some reasons why I'd prefer a battlewagon for my next sea duty. But maybe I can learn how to do a few things and pass along that information to my successor. However, it is a happy ship, and a great crew who give no trouble on liberty and who know how to conduct themselves anywhere.

Well, dear, I must get this sealed and in the mail. Lots and lots of love. The halfway mark will be more than passed when you get this, want an apartment or a house? Better persuade the family to come out for the summer and share a house with us down Belmont Shores way. Give my love to all the family.

Ever your loving hubby,

Tom

In January 1932, during one of those periods the *Saratoga* was in port, the child who was to become young Tommy was conceived. Since Genevieve had already suffered three miscarriages, this pregnancy held great hope for them. Genevieve's doctors recommended that she stay in Long Beach for her safety and that of her unborn child. Tom's next posting was to the New York Naval Shipyard, also known as the Brooklyn Navy Yard. So they went through another lengthy separation but continued to exchange letters throughout the pregnancy.

Fig. 5-1 Letter from Adm. Byrd

Fig. 5-2 Saratoga underway

Fig. 5-3 Tom before 1st Flight

Fig. 5-4 Vought O2U2 carrier aircraft on flyby of Saratoga

CHAPTER 6

Ashore Again: New York Naval Shipyard

The Brooklyn Naval Shipyard, where Tom became the base chaplain, had a long and storied history. It began in 1781 when John Jackson and his brothers built the area's first shipyard. Their new yard, still under civilian control, was commissioned in 1798 by the United Sates Government to build the USS *Adams*, a twenty-eight-gun frigate (fig. 6-1). The ship served with distinction until her crew had to burn and sink her during the War of 1812 to avoid her capture by the British.

The yard passed from civilian to government hands when the United States purchased it in 1801 from the Jackson's for the princely sum of $40,000. Operated by the Navy from that time on, the yard participated in numerous technological developments. In 1837, the yard built and launched the first steam-powered warship, the side-wheeler *Fulton II* (fig. 6-2), shortly before the naval hero Matthew C. Perry became the commandant of the yard.

In a twist of irony, the famous ironclad, the *Monitor*, was outfitted with its innovative armor at a civilian yard a short distance from the Navy yard prior to the Civil War.

In 1895, the yard launched another famous vessel, the battleship USS *Maine* (fig. 6-3), marking the beginning of what became known as "the battleship era." The *Maine* exploded mysteriously off Havana three years later, providing the spark that started the Spanish-

American War. This event gave Theodore Roosevelt and his Rough Riders their chance to become immortalized as he led the charge up San Juan Hill.

Two more famous battleships were built at the yard. In 1915, the USS *Arizona* was launched (fig. 6-4), followed in 1944 by the USS *Missouri* (fig. 6-5). As fate would have it, these two ships formed the bookends to the United States' participation in World War II. The *Arizona* was sunk during the Japanese Pearl Harbor attack, with the loss of 1,177 crewmembers, among them Chaplain Thomas L. Kirkpatrick. This unprovoked and surprise hostile action prompted President Franklin Delano Roosevelt to ask Congress for a Declaration of War the following day, thus bringing the United States into World War II. Then on September 2, 1945, in Tokyo Bay, the USS *Missouri* took part in the final act of the war as, on her main deck, officials of the Empire of Japan and representatives of the United States and our allies signed the Japanese Instrument of Surrender, ending World War II.

In 1932, Tom and Genevieve faced an agonizing decision. They agreed that Tom should follow orders and go to his new duty station in Brooklyn. He was concerned about leaving Genevieve behind, worried that the fourth pregnancy would end like the previous three. However, Tom reported for duty across the continent and Genevieve stayed in Long Beach where the doctors could monitor her closely until she gave birth. Tom sent this letter to Genevieve the day before her thirty-fourth birthday, as she waited anxiously for her baby's arrival.

August 1, 1932

My Dearest Wife:

Three letters today, and that beautiful picture. I like it immensely. When it came, I put it up on the desk in front of me, and feasted my eyes on you.

It makes me almost feel that you are here to celebrate your birthday with me. It surely was a surprise, and the most pleasant one you could have sprung on me. I hope the flowers in the morning, and the message with them, please you half as much. Also that last night's letter reaches you. I had quite a time mailing it, as I found that the nearby branch post office had the same collection as the Y, which meant none late Sunday evening. But as I was glancing at the schedule, a policeman came up to mail a letter, and he too was disappointed. So I told him I'd take him down to the main Brooklyn office if he'd guide me. And so the letter was posted and should have caught this morning's early plane.

Today has been a fine cool day, but a regular "preacher's Monday" for me. Sort of muggy, though I had enough fresh air up the Hudson. I didn't clean the windshield before starting back, and eyestrain may have caused some of today's dullness. But I brought home Sabatini's latest romance The Black Swan, *and it has helped to bear the latter part of the day.*

… As to the babe, do you mean to tell me the doctor told you whether it will be a boy or a girl, and you keep me guessing? If so, I'll say it's a boy. Right? I surely hope you won't have as many days when you feel nauseated. Didn't know that happened after the first month or so. As for a trip by air, it is as cheap as rail, and a whole lot quicker, and if any reason arose for me to come, I'd probably come that way. No, I'm not figuring on it anymore than you are, but just trying to consider all the possible contingencies. I hope and pray all will go well, as it has thus far. This is heavier paper, so I'll not risk another sheet, but I

*love you three sheets worth, and lots more. Check
also enclosed.*

Your own Tom

Genevieve had lots of support from their friends and
family while she waited in Long Beach. Many of Tom's
large Kirkpatrick clan also helped out. Tom's sister Mary,
a registered nurse, traveled cross-country to assist
Genevieve, allowing her to spend as much time as much
time as possible resting in bed. Mary was there at 5:45
a.m. on September 5, 1932, when the long-hoped for
baby arrived at Seaside Hospital. She immediately sent
Tom a telegram announcing the great event. And he
wrote a joyous letter the very same day.

September 5, 1932

My Darling,

*What a wonderful anniversary present you gave
me this time! Thomas Ivan Kirkpatrick—how does
that sound? Rather distinguished, don't you
think? It is a strange but true fact that at the very
time the boy was coming into the world, he was
being named by his father three thousand miles
away. For I was leaving Philadelphia just at 9:30
this morning and was telling Mother and Jane,
who had come down to see me off, what the name
of my son would be—if a son it were. That "my"
slipped out unconsciously, the egotism of the male
at the first son. But you'll forgive your proud papa,
won't you? I'm almost too elated to write, but I'm
going to keep on anyhow.*

*Mary's telegram was awaiting me at the desk,
when I arrived at 1:15. It didn't arrive much
before then, for it left Long Beach at 11:32 our
time. Well, I ate some lunch, sent you a telegram*

from the nearest office, phoned the good news to Mother, and have since sent out notes to all the family, including Nita. So you'll probably be getting plenty of letters soon. Needless to say, I am eagerly awaiting the details and hope Mary has sent me the airmail letter already. She didn't give me the weight in her message but he should have been a big fellow from what you have been writing. I'm wondering when you went to the hospital for this was the first message. Now that it is all over, I'm glad I didn't know, for I would have been too excited to preach, I'm afraid, if I had known you were in the hospital. Or did it all happen suddenly? Of course, I'll know when I get the letter.

Meanwhile, here's all my love, my dearest wife, and hopes and prayers that both of you will keep on doing well, as the message said was the case this morning. I'm truly grateful to God that all has gone so well. It's hard for me not to get on the passenger plane and come right out to Long Beach. But I won't, so long as all goes well. Love, hugs, kisses. At long last I can sign myself,

Papa Tom, your loving Husband

A week later, he wrote another letter to Genevieve from the Brooklyn Shipyard.

September 12, 1932

Dearest:

One week old today. Think he has grown any? As a matter of fact babies lose a bit the first few weeks, don't they? It surely was good to get your letter today, and hear directly from you. Mary has been a dear, but after all no letter can take the place of yours. When you mentioned that milk had just begun to flow, I was surprised, for I had supposed nature arranged all that. I'll bet Tommy was hungry, was he? So Aunt Hattie said that he looks like his daddy at his age—poor baby.

Well, maybe he'll improve with age. Hope so? Just the same, I'm glad he looks like me. Mary says she can't see the resemblance, but that Ann Dittman said he took after his daddy. I'm surely happy that you have so many friends nearby to drop in to see you.... Had a note today from L. R. who said he had just phoned to Lola, so she could write you. I'll send his on when I've answered it. Also had a note from Rube, so I imagine you'll hear from Alma. It is great to be opening letters of congratulations on the arrival of a son. I'll tell the World!!

... The moon shines on just the same, even better than last week for it is almost full. If its beams shine in your room they'll bring you my message of love.

Tommy's Dad and Your Loving Hubby

On September 14, Captain Harold R. Stark, at that time aide to the secretary of the Navy, sent a short letter of congratulations to the new parents (fig. 6-6). Captain Stark later became Admiral Stark, and, in a twist of irony, was chief of naval operations in charge of the Navy at the time of the Pearl Harbor attack that took the life of his friend. He unfortunately became embroiled in the heated controversy surrounding the search for the guilty, as Congress and others looked for someone to blame for the United States' being caught flat-footed by the Japanese attack.

As soon as it was safe for Genevieve to travel with newborn Tommy, she boarded a train in Los Angeles and headed east. After the reunion and introduction of son to father, the couple settled down to a more normal domestic life in Brooklyn. Genevieve managed the day-to-day household tasks in addition to tending to the baby's needs while Tom continued his duties as the base chaplain, conducting church services in the chapel, visiting men in the base hospital, and counseling those in need. In figure 6-7 he is presenting a Bible in Armenian to a man who was born near the biblical Mount Ararat. He described the event:

> *The chaplain at the Naval Hospital, Brooklyn, gets a lesson in Armenian when he presents a gospel in Armenian to one who was born in the region of Mt. Ararat. Among the thousand patients, there are always a number who are more at home when they can read the Bible in Greek, Armenian, Italian, or Yiddish.*

As a Navy chaplain, Tom was charged with seeing to the spiritual and counseling needs of a flock consisting of men from diverse backgrounds, races, ethnicities, and religions. In fact, Tom had learned some Armenian, as well as Turkish and Farsi, when he was a missionary in Tabriz, Persia, from 1911–1914, and he could carry on a conversation in both German and French as well. By his own statement, he also knew a "smattering" of Sanskrit.

It didn't hurt if a chaplain also had a good sense of humor. In figure 6-8, Tom is joking with a group of patients. His description of this scene includes an elaborate story:

> *The chaplain interrupts a card game at the Naval Hospital to tell the old yarn about a sailor who*

was arrested in a strict New England hamlet because he was looking through a deck of playing cards during the church service. His defense before the judge was that when he was on a long voyage and was without a Bible, a pack of cards could serve as such, "For when I see the ace," he said, "I am reminded that there is but one God. The deuce reminds me that the Bible is divided into two parts, the Old and the New Testament. The three-spot recalls to my mind the doctrine of the Trinity; the four, the Four Gospels; and the five, the five wise men and five foolish virgins. The six-spot recalls to my mind the creation of the universe, and the seven, God's provision of one day in seven for worship and rest. An eight brings to mind the story of the Flood, in which eight persons only were saved in the Ark. Nine becomes a lesson in gratitude, for of ten lepers once healed by our Lord, nine went ungratefully on their way, while only one turned back to thank Jesus. The ten-spot is a lesson in morality, for it recalls the Ten Commandments. The queen brings to mind the visit by the Queen of Sheba to wise King Solomon. The king brings me back again to thoughts of God Almighty, the King of Kings and Lord of Lords, the Creator and Ruler of the Universe." When he paused the judge said, "You have left out one card, the jack." To which the sailor answered, "Meaning no disrespect to you, sir, the jack, which is often called the knave, reminds me of the Evil One, whose servant it must have been who brought me here."

The Navy is well-known for moving people around. With such an ever-changing flock, it might seem the pastoral task of a chaplain would be an exercise in frustration. Tom had a different take on the situation. In figure 6-9, Tom is shown meeting an old friend, a former shipmate. He described the event:

Chaplain Kirkpatrick meets an old shipmate in a ward of the Naval Hospital, Brooklyn, and supplies him with a Bible furnished by the American Bible Society. Though a chaplain changes duty about every two years, he keeps meeting old friends who have also moved from ship to ship, or to shore duty, and his pastoral work thus tends to have somewhat of a cumulative influence comparable to that of a minister in a civilian parish. Of the thousand patients in this hospital in 1933 a large majority are World War veterans, hospitalized by the Veterans' Bureau.

Figures 6-10 and 6-11 tell the story better than words, as Tom holds his newborn son for the first time. Figure 6-12 shows how much his proud and relieved parents wanted, loved, and cherished their son. Tom could not resist taking the typical "bearskin rug" picture of little Tommy (fig. 6-13) or of Tommy in the bathtub (fig. 6-14). He could hardly wait to show off his son to the family, so he invited his mother to Brooklyn for a visit. Figure 6-15 shows all three generations—infant son, mother and father, and Grandmother Kirkpatrick—posed by the ancient cannon displayed ceremonially on the grounds of the Brooklyn Navy Yard.

Tom's sister, Mary, who had helped so much toward the end of Genevieve's pregnancy, came for a visit with her daughter Jane Willets. Figure 6-16 depicts the proud Papa, Jane holding Tommy, Mary standing behind Jane with Mrs. Kirkpatrick to the right, and to the far right, Genevieve positively beams. Of course, Tom had to introduce his new son to his old and dear friends as well (fig. 6-17). On the left is Chaplain Robert D. Workman, who became chief of chaplains in 1937. On the right is Chaplain Razzie W. Truitt, who was a classmate of Tom's in Chaplain School in 1918. Tommy later called Chaplain Truitt his "Uncle Razzie."

However, it was not all so much fun. During their stay in Brooklyn, an epidemic of pertussis, better known as whooping cough, struck. It's not clear who came down with it first, but both Big Tom and Little Tommie were deathly ill with it at the same time. Genevieve would later tell of her great concern while trying to nurse both back to health. Fortunately, she was able to avoid being infected herself. She described the constant racking cough both were plagued with – endless deep and hard coughing fits - followed by the sufferer's gasping for breath, making the characteristic whooping sound that gave the disease its name. Today, we tend to think of pertussis as just another childhood disease, but it is a good deal more. Patients used to die from it, especially children. Among families who have their children inoculated with the DPT vaccine, the disease has ceased to be a threat. However, among those families who have chosen not to use the vaccine, serious illness and sometimes death can still occur.

Then, on January 22, 1935, Tom received orders detaching him from his duty at the Brooklyn Navy Yard as of May 2, 1935. He was ordered to a most unusual duty station: the Pago Pago Navy Base on the island of Tutuila, American Samoa. This tropical island group lies in the middle of the vast Pacific Ocean halfway between Hawaii and Australia, roughly 2,500 miles from each. After a lengthy trip by transcontinental train, then by steamer across the Pacific, Tom reported on June 8, 1935. This turned out to be one of his most interesting assignments, one where he had a chance to study the fascinating traditional culture of Samoa. Despite the many difficulties in traveling around the island, he took full advantage of the opportunity as he discharged not only the normal duties of being a base chaplain but also superintendent of Samoan Schools. This latter duty required him to oversee and regularly inspect the numerous village schools the Navy had established to teach something like a mainland curriculum to Samoan children. The move was challenging for Genevieve too as she tried to maintain a more or less normal lifestyle for her family in a place so totally different from anything she had ever experienced.

Fig. 6-1 *U.S.S. Adams* 28-gun frigate commissioned by U.S. Government in 1798.

Fig. 6-2 *U.S.S. Fulton* Built in 1837, shown after reconstruction in 1851.

Fig. 6-3 *U.S.S. Maine* Built in 1895, ship exploded in Havana, starting Spanish-
American War in 1898.

Fig. 6-4 U.S.S. Arizona Shown at her launching in 1915.

Fig. 6-5 U.S.S. Missouri Launched in 1944, she ended WW-II in Tokyo Bay.

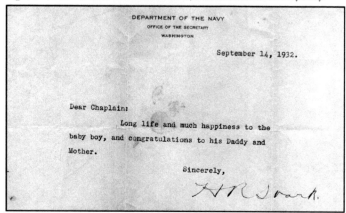

Fig. 6-6 Letter from Captain Harold R. Stark Later, Admiral and CNO in 1941.

Fig. 6-7 Presenting Armenian Bible

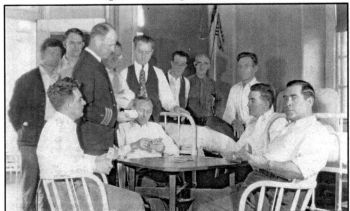

Fig. 6-8 Biblical Card Trick How to tell a Bible Story with a deck of cards.

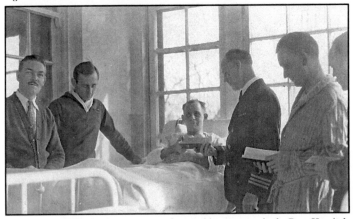

Fig. 6-9 An Old Friend Tom meets a former shipmate, now in the Base Hospital.

Fig. 6-10 Tom meets Tommy   Fig. 6-11 Tommy meets Chaplain

Fig. 6-12 Mutual Admiration Society Well, almost.

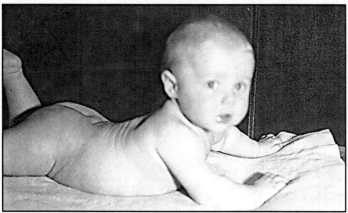

Fig. 6-13 Did Daddy really take my picture? Like this? I'll never live it down!

Fig. 6-14 This thing is cold!

Fig. 6-15 Three Generations Daddy, Tommy, Mommy, Grandma K., and a cannon.

Fig. 6-16 Cousin Jane holds Tommy   *Fig. 6-17 Chaplains Workman , Truitt*

CHAPTER 7

Something Completely Different: Pago Pago Navy Base, Island of Tutuila, American Samoa

Tom's next assignment was one both he and Genevieve considered out of the ordinary for a Navy chaplain at the time, though not at all unwelcome. The islands of American Samoa, formerly colonized by Germany, had been ceded to the United States as part of the treaty ending World War I. When the Kirkpatrick family arrived, the native population still practiced a great deal of the traditional Samoan culture. The United States felt Samoa's location in the South Pacific was strategic enough to establish a naval base in Pago Pago Harbor on the island of Tutuila, and they maintained a significant presence there. Air travel was yet to come to this remote part of the world, so travel and commerce between Samoa and the American mainland was primarily by the steam-powered passenger ships of the Matson Lines, which is how the family made the lengthy trip from the mainland to this exotic outpost. The trip included a brief stopover in Honolulu, where Matson had established what had become the world-famous and iconic hotel, the Royal Hawaiian, known affectionately as The Pink Palace.

And so, on a hot and beautiful day in 1935, the SS *Lurline* (fig. 7-1), pride of the Matson Lines, glided majestically into Pago Pago Harbor. *Fautasi*, Samoan for longboats (fig. 7-2), manned by sturdy Samoan oarsmen, shoved off from shore to meet the ship after it had anchored in the center of the bay, their job to ferry passengers and cargo between ship and shore. Depending on where the passengers were to disembark, the oarsmen would carry their passengers to dry land (fig. 7-3). Even the governor needed this service at times (fig. 7-4). As Tom described it:

> *The way we do it in Samoa: Governor Dowling being carried to the fautasi at Olosega. Here's where the Samoan fashion of lavalava, which can be tucked up, and no shoes, comes in handy.*

From the upper deck of the ship, a little boy not yet three years of age watched in fascination, flanked by his parents, Chaplain and Mrs. Thomas L. Kirkpatrick. The family spent over two years living in this tropical paradise, the elder Kirkpatrick acting as the base chaplain for the U.S. Naval Base at Pago Pago.

Samoa was picture-perfect with miles and miles of snow-white beaches (fig. 7-5), coconut palms arching out over the sand, crystal clear water, waves breaking over the barrier reefs, and gentle tropical breezes blowing. Pago Pago Harbor (fig. 7-6) was formed by the collapse of one wall of an ancient volcanic caldera (fig. 7-7), which allowed the sea to flow in and fill the crater. This became what was renowned as the finest deepwater harbor in the South Pacific. The remainder of the caldera formed a ring of high mountains surrounding the harbor, except for the seaward opening. On the east side of the bay, a particularly spectacular peak rose, known for generations as Mount Rainmaker. The moisture-laden tropical air blew across it, which created rain clouds that then dumped their load onto the island every afternoon.

The family lived in a tin-roofed house, supplied by the Navy, on "Centipede Row" alongside the homes of other Naval officers and their families (fig. 7-8). The house was raised on stilts, each of their bases enclosed by a large can filled with water, which prevented the incursion of various nasty critters, most notable among them being the very large and ill-tempered centipedes that abounded. The only critters more numerous than the centipedes and their cousins were the mosquitoes. To mount a defense against egg-laying by these voracious bloodsuckers, the surface of each miniature moat was covered with a thin layer of kerosene.

The houses along Centipede Row each had a large screened porch around three sides. This served as a primitive form of air conditioning, giving some relief from the heat and humidity. To counter the daily rains supplied courtesy of Mount Rainmaker, families mounted canvas curtains on cables at the top and bottom of the screened openings. When the afternoon rains came, these curtains were hurriedly drawn. Oddly enough, this daily ritual seemed to take place in an atmosphere of mild panic, as though the rain was unexpected. In fact, you could have set your watch by the onset of the day's rainfall.

As Tom and Genevieve settled into their new home, they fell into a routine again. Figure 7-9 shows Tom delivering what he liked to refer to as a "chalk talk" at evening Vespers. In addition to this type of ecclesiastical duty, Tom was the superintendent of Schools for the native Samoan population. He periodically inspected the schools where Samoan children were taught basic English, as well as the rest of the curriculum taught in mainland public schools (fig. 7-10). There was one problem: transportation. The schools were located in the numerous villages scattered around the coast of the island. They were accessible only by taking an outrigger canoe (fig. 7-11) through the reef, paddling around the island to the next village, then coming back to the beach through gaps in the reef. Nevertheless, Tom enjoyed these trips immensely, even when arriving at his destination a wee bit soggy. He realized there was a great deal to be admired in the Samoans' traditional culture—the ceremonies, the song and dance, even their method of building—so he strongly encouraged its preservation, while at the same time exposing the Samoan children to the wider influences of the outside world.

Samoans placed great importance upon ceremony. Whenever a visitor of rank arrived at a village, the elders and chiefs were required to greet him with an appropriately dignified formality known as the kava ceremony. By way of comparison, the Japanese have a similar ritual known as the tea ceremony. Kava is a liquid derived from the kava root (fig. 7-12). It was chopped and ground finely, and then specially selected men of the village brewed it into a reddish-brownish liquid that to non-Samoans tasted something like rusty water. It has mildly psychoactive properties alleged to produce a relaxed and receptive state, but without the mental stupor associated with alcohol consumption. It was served from a kava bowl (fig. 7-13) using cups made of coconut shell. Designated helpers served the honored visitor first, then the rest in order of rank and importance.

In addition to the kava ceremony, the elders and chiefs, such as this high chief, or *Matai* (fig. 7-14), with his staff of rank greeted the visitor. Talking chiefs, *Tulafale* (fig. 7-15), delivered speeches of welcome. These men are shown wearing lavalavas made of traditional tapa cloth, also called siapo. It was fashioned of layers of beaten and expanded inner bark of the mulberry tree, usually three layers with fibers laid in a crossing pattern. Once dried, the cloth was decorated in traditional patterns, using native dyes. The decoration was applied both freehand and by using carved hardwood boards moistened with dye and pressed against the cloth.

Samoans also loved to sing and dance, so on some occasions, there was entertainment, such as the sitting dancers who used only their expressive and graceful hand and arm motions (fig. 7- 16) and groups of siva siva dancers (fig. 7-17, 7-18). It was a longstanding Samoan tradition that the host family prepared food and lodging for the extended family and guests at important celebrations. An important part of the feast was the roasting of pigs in fire pits (fig. 7-19). Tom described the scene:

> *Some of the roast pigs, which were divided among the guests at the Mauga ceremonies, November 30, 1935. All were first laid out so that everyone could see the number, and then a talking chief presided at the distribution.*

To accompany singing, the Samoans used a unique type of drum, shaped like the one shown in figure 7-20. This one was carved from a single log, and was struck with the large pole that is sticking up from the central cavity. Even the small handheld versions of such drums could make a prodigious sound when struck, so this large example must have reverberated loud and far.

The pride in home and family carried over to the Samoan dwellings, which were built in oval or round shapes, with thatched roofs as seen in figures 7-21 and 7-22. Floors were made of coral rubble, and the peripheral openings were fitted with woven mats or tapa cloths that could be rolled down between the timber support posts to provide shelter from the elements, or rolled up to allow for air circulation. The thatched roofs were shaped and supported by elaborately built structures as shown in figure 7-23. Tom described this scene:

A glimpse from floor to roof, or ceiling of a fale. Not a nail used, but all beams and posts and battens held together by cords of sennit, of coconut fibre, often adjusted in very intricate and beautiful patterns. Posts of any hardwood, rafters of breadfruit tree, battens of bamboo in most cases.

Samoans prized craftsmanship, and the skilled and highly paid craftsmen were organized into guilds. Figure 7-24 shows two men making and joining beams. Tom described this scene:

Carpenter (left) joining together sections of a curved rafter for a "fale fale." He is using a foreign clamp of iron, but hidden by this is the real Samoan "clamp," a bit of twine around the rafter with wedges driven under to tighten it. These are left in place until the rafter is in place, and roof battens fastened to rafters with sennit. Twisting the sennit from fibres, after these have been obtained from coconut husks, is the most tedious part of building operations. This is done by the village matais at odd times. The actual carpentering is done by guilds of craftsmen who are highly regarded and well paid in Samoan fashion.

Samoans also prized competitive sports. Figure 7-25 shows a spirited tug of war between two powerful teams. Muscles bulged and backs strained to see which team could pull the other across the line under the watchful eyes of the judges, while being urged passionately to exert even greater effort by their supporters.

A tropical climate includes humidity. As American mainlanders, Tom and Genevieve arrived at Pago Pago equipped with shoes and other goods made of leather. In a place like Samoa, such items immediately become a feeding ground for a plethora of fungi. In order to combat this effect, each of the Centipede Row houses was equipped with a special space called the "hot closet." This was a cedar-lined walk-in room where electric light bulbs were lit 24/7. This additional heat was effective at keeping vulnerable items dry enough to forestall the otherwise inevitable rot.

And then ... the centipede problem. It was real, as Tom found out to his dismay one evening. While pulling open the dinner table to insert an extra leaf, he chanced to curl his fingers underneath the apron around its edge. An immediate loud cry was followed by various muffled groans and mumblings as he valiantly suppressed the utterance of words simply not heard to pass the lips of a man of God. It turned out his hand had impinged upon the space previously claimed by a very large, very black, very venomous centipede that had somehow crossed the miniature moats beneath the house. This creature expressed its extreme displeasure by inflicting a savage bite upon the intruder. Tom spent the next two weeks nursing a hand that looked more like a ham, both in size and color, than a human appendage.

As January 16, 1936, dawned, Genevieve announced to Tommy that they were going on an adventure together. He thought she meant one of their usual bicycle rides around Pago Pago Harbor. To his surprise the ride ended at the Naval base. It turned out there was a compelling reason for the abrupt termination to the "adventure." The base was the only reinforced concrete structure on the island, and it was the only refuge deemed safe enough for the Navy families when the fast-approaching hurricane struck. It can be seen in this view of the base, between the docked ship and the radio tower (fig. 7-26, 7-27). Tom described these pictures:

Looking east at the main body of the U.S. Naval Station buildings. Radio towers 420 feet high work with Honolulu regularly. The British gunboat Leith *at dock. This visit of a foreign man-of-war is a pleasant interlude two or three times each year.*

The hurricane of 1936 struck with the usual sound and fury, inflicting major damage on the island. The Navy family members all had vivid memories of sleeping on canvas cots in a large, high-ceilinged room alongside dozens of other women and children, the men quartered in a separate room. It was dark, spooky, and eerily quiet, even though the hurricane raged just outside.

The following morning, the families emerged from their safe haven and returned to Centipede Row. The houses were, for the most part, still standing. Figures 7-28, 7-29, 7-30, and 7-31 show part of the devastation to both American-style structures and Samoan fale fales. Most of their roofs were displaced. A few still had most of the roofing attached, all rolled up into giant tin tubes. Their interiors resembled swimming pools on stilts. Trees lay on the ground. Palm fronds decorated the landscape. Household furniture and possessions were a soggy, putrid mess.

Centipede Row was located a short distance from the shore of Pago Pago Bay. In front of the houses was a path of coral rubble. At the southern end of this path, a concrete pier jutted out into the bay, concrete steps descending into the water from its side. On that same side, sturdy hurricane fencing had been installed in the water, enclosing a large rectangular area. This space was for the swimming pleasure of the officers and their families. One could look down into the crystalline water and see the bottom, resplendent in its brilliant hues of coral and marine growth, equally brilliant tropical fish swimming about. The reason for the hurricane fencing around the swimming pool became abundantly clear when, on occasion, a large fin could be seen protruding above the surface, whipping rapidly back and forth just outside the fencing. It didn't take much imagination to understand the need for the protected enclosure.

Samoan children learned to swim almost before they could walk. When a Samoan family traveled to visit relatives in another village, they had to do so by outrigger canoe. Upsets and swampings were frequent when negotiating the reef, so it was imperative that everyone in the canoe be a competent swimmer, including very young children. Many American families hired Samoan household help such as nannies to look after their children. Occasionally, the cultural differences could lead to misunderstandings, like a nanny taking the very young children in her charge swimming, causing great concern on the part of the typically overprotective American mothers.

The two cultures came together when the Navy, with the cooperation of Samoan leaders, formed a native regiment called the Fita Fita Guard. This unit took part in numerous ceremonial duties (fig. 7-32) including a parade at the Pago Pago Naval Base (fig. 7-33). Tommy's parents gave him a miniature copy of the Fita Fita Guard's dress uniform including a lavalava. The Guard wore more or less standard Navy attire above the lavalava. As the base chaplain, Tom was expected to attend these events. On one such occasion, the family attended, Tom in uniform, Genevieve in the standard white linen dress, and Tommy in his tiny Fita Fita Guard outfit. The band played Sousa music, the Guard marched smartly, and the appreciative crowd applauded the marvelous spectacle. This excitement proved too much for Tommy to resist. He suddenly dashed out onto the parade ground and proceeded to march along behind the Fita Fita Guard regiment. That is until a pair of local mongrels, similarly excited, decided that the hem of his lavalava was too much to resist. They grabbed the hem and started pulling and tugging. Tommy was infuriated at the audacity of the dogs as they tried their best to render him bare-bottom naked, and in front of the whole assemblage, too. So he fought back, leaning and twisting frantically about, trying to loose their grip on the lavalava. No use. They won. So, there he was, lying on the ground, undressed, legs flailing in the air, kicking and screaming in frustration and humiliation.

However, the story didn't end there. The Fita Fita Guard had crisply performed an about-face maneuver and was marching directly back toward the distressed boy. Samoans are descendants of fierce ancient warriors (fig. 7-34) and these men resembled their ancestors. But, at the tender age of three and a half, Tommy was too distressed and angry to speculate about the possibility of being trampled by the whole regiment. So, he lay there, the ground quaking beneath him, as the files of men parted just enough to pass on both sides, ignoring the piteous wails. When they had safely passed, an adult ran out, mercifully swooped Tommy up, and carried him to safety, still minus the lavalava and still very unhappy.

Again because of his position, Tom and Genevieve were regular invitees to dinner parties hosted by Governor and Mrs. Dowling in the Gubernatorial Mansion (fig. 7-35) overlooking the harbor entrance. These events were always of great social significance, and Mrs. Dowling spared no expense or trouble to set forth a sumptuous repast. Genevieve loved to tell the story of one particular evening. Mrs. Dowling had received an iced shipment of lettuce, delivered during the latest visit of a Matson Lines ship. As a special treat, she had her Samoan chef make a giant bowl of tossed green salad, a true delicacy for that climate. Her guests helped themselves liberally and seemed to enjoy it immensely. That is until IT happened.

The lushness of Samoa comes complete with exotic flora and fauna such as the gecko. These agile lizard-like creatures have sticky pads on their toes, and they particularly like to climb around inside houses. Unfortunately, that day, one had lost its grip on the governor's kitchen ceiling, falling to its demise inside the bowl of lettuce, unnoticed by the chef. Then IT happened: a dinner guest encountered the corpus delecti among the greens, which elicited a chandelier-rattling screech. The vocal alarm had the electrifying effect of alerting her fellow diners that their portion of salad might be hiding something horrible as well. This revelation resulted in a period of mad scrambling while all of the guests pawed frantically through their own plates, just in case.

On March 12, 1937, the Samoan adventure ended. Tom received orders detaching him from his duties in Samoa and sending him back home to the mainland where he became the base chaplain at the Marine Corps Barracks in San Diego. Tom and Genevieve would be returning to a familiar and congenial community where they had made many friends while Tom was stationed at the Naval Training Center next door. The family immediately booked passage on the next Matson Lines steamer and set about packing for the trip home.

Finally, the day of the family's return to the mainland arrived. Well-wishers, both Samoans and mainlanders, placed many leis about their necks (fig. 7-36), sang songs of parting, shared hugs, and escorted them to their fautasi. The Samoan oarsmen pulled the longboat smartly out across Pago Pago Harbor to the SS *Matsonia*, anchored in the center of the bay, then helped the travelers up the gangway. Tom, Genevieve, and Tommy were on their way home (fig. 7-37).

The experience of becoming immersed in the Samoan culture made a deep impression on Tom. He had always been a people person and in many ways an amateur anthropologist. He thoroughly enjoyed his school inspection sojourns around Tutuila by outrigger canoe, seeing firsthand the traditional lifestyle, experiencing various ceremonies, even taking part in some. He always carried his camera and asked a lot of questions, recording his travels and observations both in writing and in the many photographs he took. For the rest of his life, he maintained a deep and abiding love and respect for the people he had befriended and for the ancient Samoan culture, one rich in values, with strong family ties, and sense of duty paramount. Like the Samoans, Tom was devoted to his large extended family and even larger company of friends and colleagues, making him the favorite "Uncle Roy" to all.

Fig. 7-1 S.S. Lurline in Pago Pago

Fig. 7-2 Samoan longboat "Fautasi" transported passengers and goods to shore.

Fig. 7-3 Landing, Samoan Style Samoans carried passengers from boat to dry land.

Fig. 7-4 Governor Dowling boards his special Fautasi the Samoan way

Fig. 7-5 Samoan beach scene   *Fig. 7-6 Pago Pago Harbor*

Fig. 7-7 Pago Pago Harbor Volcanic shoreline, typical small Samoan canoe.

Fig. 7-8 Centipede Row House Home of Chaplain Kirkpatrick and family.

Fig. 7-9 The Chaplain delivers a "chalk talk" at evening vespers

Fig. 7-10 Samoan School Typical of schools in Samoan villages around Tutuila.

Fig. 7-11 Large outrigger canoe

Fig. 7-12 Kava Root being harvested

Fig. 7-13 The Kava Ceremony Typical Kava bowl on mat at right.

Fig. 7-14 Matai A High Chief

Fig. 7-15 Talking Chiefs With their fly whisks of office over their shoulders.

Fig. 7-16 Women performing a sitting dance Using graceful hand and arm motions.

Fig. 7-17 Siva Siva Dancers

Fig. 7-18 Siva Siva Dancers at wedding

Fig. 7-19 Distribution of Roast Pigs at wedding Talking Chiefs are presiding.

Fig. 7-20   Samoan long range drum

Fig. 7-21   Typical Samoan Fale

Fig. 7-22   Typical Small Samoan Village

Fig. 7-23   Fale Fale interior view

Fig. 7-24   Carpenters Guild craftsmen at Work

Fig. 7-25 Tug-of-War competition

Fig. 7-26 Pago Pago Naval Base Concrete building at left. radio tower at right.

Fig. 7-27 420-foot radio tower

Fig. 7-28 1936 hurricane's damage School Principal's roof 1/4 mile up mountain.

Fig. 7-29 Hurricane damage School Superintendent's roof blown off.

Fig. 7-30 Shallow soil allowed trees to be blown over

Fig. 7-31 Hurricane blew half of roof off Fale Fale

Fig. 7-32 Fita Fita Guard Honor guard for an official welcoming ceremony.

Fig. 7-33 Fita Fita Guard on parade

Fig. 7-34 Young Samoan Man

Fig. 7-35 Governor's Mansion

Fig. 7-36 Samoan Farewell Leis, called ulas in Samoa, drape recipients.

Fig. 7-37 Family aboard Matsonia

CHAPTER 8

Stateside Again

Tom, Genevieve, and Tommy arrived in San Diego in time for Tom to report on April 20, 1937, for duty at the Marine Corps Barracks as it was then called. Nowadays it is called Marine Corps Recruit Depot, MCRD for short. It is one of two basic training facilities for immersing new recruits in the ways of the Marine Corps, the other being in Parris Island, South Carolina. MCRD San Diego also trains the legendary Marine Corps Drill Sergeants. New recruits get supplementary training in field skills at Camp Pendleton in the North County, then return to San Diego for The Crucible, a grueling fifty-four-hour "final exam," designed to be the final weeding out stage.

When the depot was built in the '20s, a California Spanish architectural style was adopted, with liberal use of stucco, red tile roofs, and long covered walkways, called arcades. One of these was a half-mile long and linked a row of the original buildings facing a large parade ground.

While serving at MCRD, Tom adopted a Marine Corps uniform and the rank of lt. colonel, equivalent to his Navy rank of commander. His duties were very much like they had been at the Naval Training Center earlier in his career. He preached the gospel at the base chapel, officiated at ceremonial occasions by giving the invocations, and counseled base personnel. In a letter to Genevieve in May of 1941, Tom compared his typical day counseling personnel aboard ship to his counseling load at MCRD, which was much heavier. One can speculate that the severe demands deliberately made on Marine recruits might have exacerbated the personal and family problems they experienced.

Tom and Genevieve were expected to lead an active social schedule, entertaining the families of fellow officers as well as the occasional group of recruits, and taking part in various on-base activities. Tom also performed the same kind of interfacing to the community of San Diego as he had at the Naval Training Center.

The couple's tour at the Marine Corps Barracks was one period when life was easy and congenial for them; they even had the opportunity to travel as a family. Unlike their earlier experience with house hunting, they quickly found a comfortable residence at 3030 Dumas Street in Loma Portal, one-half block from the Naval Training Center and just a short distance from the main gate of the Marine Corps Barracks. Tommy attended the local school, within easy walking distance from the house. In figure 8-1, he is standing in front of this house with his cousin Phyllis Childs. She later broke professional ground by graduating with her M.D. from Woman's Medical College of Pennsylvania in Philadelphia and going on to practice medicine for a number of years in Southern California.

On Sunday after church, the rest of the day was generally devoted to entertaining a number of guests at a large afternoon dinner, using the home's ample dining room. This was a rather formal affair; Tom stood at the head of the table while Genevieve brought the lovingly prepared roast beef or roasted turkey from the kitchen. Tom would then say grace and carve the meat, putting slices on the plates the guests passed down the table to him. Tom's outgoing and welcoming nature always made guests feel welcome and at ease.

San Diego had numerous opportunities for recreation, both on land and in the water. As seen in figures 8-2 and 8-3, the Kirkpatrick family spent a lot of time at Mission Beach, enjoying its miles of broad white sand. The world-famous San Diego Zoo held many attractions for the family, as Tommy is seen in figure 8-4 flanking an elephant with Jim Woods, a cousin visiting from Colorado. The family also visited the famous Hotel Del Coronado, known to locals affectionately as the Hotel Del (fig. 8-5). It lies at the north end of a fabulous beach known as the Silver Strand. A bit further from home, they traveled to the Mount Palomar Observatory shown in figure 8-6 under construction, being readied to house the world's largest reflecting telescope.

The family took several long-distance vacations as well. They drove to the High Sierras (fig. 8-7, 8-8), Yosemite Valley (fig. 8-9, 8-10, 8-11), Death Valley, the Petrified Forest, Grand Canyon (fig. 8-12, 8-13), Bryce Canyon (fig. 8-14), and they took the steamer to Catalina Island. Visiting relatives formed an important part of the family's life as well. Tom always made an effort to stay in touch with his extended family, all adored him and looked up to him as the family's favorite uncle and elder. Tommy's cousin, Dr. Phyllis Moeller (née: Childs), now retired, recently said, "Uncle Roy was the nicest person you would ever want to meet—and he was so much *fun!*"

One of their trips was a family get-together in Gold Hill, Colorado, where Tommy was introduced to horseback riding. In figure 8-15, he is out for a ride, seated in front of a cowboy. The young lady on the right was Tommy's first cousin Jane Willets. Years later, while conducting research for her advanced degree in anthropology, she met and married a full-blooded chief of the Little Traverse Bay Band of Odawa Indians in Michigan, Fred Ettawageshik. He was, along with many of his tribe, a passionate conservationist, and preached the tribal credo that when making decisions affecting the environment, one must think about the consequences seven generations ahead. Their son, Frank, also a passionate conservationist, is credited with single-handedly keeping alive an ancient form of stoneware pottery-making practiced by his Odawa ancestors, practicing and teaching the techniques.

In late 1940, the family was reminded that, as is the way in military life, no posting lasts forever. It all came to an end on August 19, 1940, when Tom received orders detaching him from MCRD San Diego and ordering him to another period of sea duty, this time as fate would have it, aboard battleship BB-39, the USS *Arizona*. In preparation for sea duty, the family packed up most of their household belongings and put them in storage. The lease on the house at 3030 Dumas expired, so they moved to a temporarily rented cottage near the sea in Mission Beach. Tommy enjoyed playing in the surf, building sand castles, and all the other things youngsters do at the beach.

When Tom reported aboard *Arizona* on September 13, 1940, the ship was at Pearl Harbor. Genevieve and Tommy remained behind on the mainland, living in their cottage at San Diego's Mission Beach. The plan was to stay until a move could be arranged to another Navy town, Long Beach, where it was expected the *Arizona* would return from time to time. That way the family could spend time together during the ship's visits. However, plans change, as happens in the Navy. *Arizona's* first West Coast trip was not to Long Beach, but to Bremerton, Washington, where she was due for an overhaul at the Puget Sound Navy Yard. Accordingly, Genevieve and Tommy moved from Mission Beach to a rented house on a peninsula jutting into one of the many inlets lining Puget Sound.

While the ship was in dry dock, Tom lived in this rented home with the family. The house fronted on a narrow road that allowed access to the peninsula, where a number of homes were located. At the rear of the house, down a steep, wooded backyard, the brackish water of Puget Sound rose and fell with the tides. Crabs crawled over the rocky bottom of the inlet at low tide. Tommy entered third grade at a public school. The family celebrated their last Christmas together in that house.

During this period Tom wrote a letter to his sister Bertha describing the home and something of their life there.

We are located on an arm of the Sound, in the midst of beautiful scenery, but haven't been able to enjoy it as we had hoped because one of the three of us has had a cold or flu most of the time. If they hadn't been having it in California, we would think that it was the colder climate and the rain, but we can't lay it to that cause. Tommy is just getting over his second siege with it, and we hope that our last few weeks here will see us able to enjoy the colder weather and get up to Mt. Rainier, and around to some of the other scenic spots hereabout.

The family eventually enjoyed the magnificent scenery of the Northwest, driving to places such as Mt. Rainier. Their drive up the winter wonderland of Mt. Rainier stopped short of their destination because of a heavy snowstorm that Tom worried might strand them unless they turned back. He continued driving the family to other places in the region, trying to make as much use of the time as he could before *Arizona's* overhaul was completed.

One of these trips provided more excitement than expected. On November 7, 1940, Tom was driving the family on a day outing in their 1937 Chevrolet sedan. The route home to Bremerton took them across the Tacoma Narrows Bridge, the third longest suspension bridge in the world at that time. The structure had been open for only a few months and it had already been nicknamed "Galloping Gertie" because of the bothersome movement of the roadbed at times. On that day Tom was having great difficulty steering the Chevy across the bridge, and he complained vociferously about it the rest of the way home. He was shocked to read the news reports the following day. Hours after the family's uncomfortable ride across the bridge a severe storm hit, which blew stiff winds directly across the roadbed. The gale eventually caused the suspension cables to snap, plunging the roadbed and everything on it into the frigid waters of Puget Sound two hundred feet below. At dinner that evening, in addition to the usual grace, Tom gave a grateful prayer of thanksgiving to God for guiding them on that trip. As a result of the catastrophe, bridge design was forever altered as engineers awakened to the fact that aerodynamic forces could seriously affect even a massive structure like a bridge.

During those years, a remarkable automobile ferry plied the waters of Puget Sound between Seattle and Bremerton, used by thousands of Navy Yard workers to commute to work daily. Named the *Kalakala*, which meant "Flying Bird" in the local Chinook language, this vessel was the world's first streamlined ferry, an amazing art-deco-style ship, smoothly rounded, painted silver, with a propulsion system that could achieve 18 knots while carrying 85 autos and as many as 5,000 passengers. Tom took the family on an outing aboard *Kalakala* one day, a thrilling event Tommy remembered well because of the heavy vibration that could be felt throughout the ship while underway.

In early February of 1940, the *Arizona's* great weight still rested upon a number of massive blocks arranged underneath the hull in the huge concrete canyon known as a dry dock. Overhaul complete, the Navy began pumping water back into the dry dock. As the water slowly rose, the great ship began to float once again. When the filling operation was complete, the heavy lock doors separating the dry dock's interior from the waters outside swung ponderously open. The USS *Arizona* eased back into Puget Sound, ready to rejoin her sister ships in Battleship Division One at Pearl Harbor.

Fig. 8-1 Tommy and Phyllis at 3030 Dumas

Fig. 8-2 Genevieve and Tommy at Mission Beach

Fig. 8-3 Genevieve and Tom at Mission Beach

Fig. 8-4 Tommy and Cousin Jim Woods At San Diego Zoo framing an elephant.

Fig. 8-5 In front of Hotel Del Coronado The "Hotel Del" to San Diegans.

Fig. 8-6 Tom, Genevieve and Tommy Palomar Observatory in background.

Fig. 8-7 In the giant Sequoias

Fig. 8-8 Lost in giant's roots

Fig. 8-9 Tom's photo of the iconic view entering Yosemite Valley

Fig. 8-10 The family standing at Yosemite's entrance overlook

Fig. 8-11 Yosemite's Mirror Lake

Fig. 8-12 Genevieve and Tom at Grand Canyon south rim

Fig. 8-13 Inspecting a daredevil's boat Used to run Colorado River rapids.

Fig. 8-14 Tom's photo of Bryce Canyon

Fig. 8-15 At Gold Hill, Colorado Tommy at left with cowboy, Cousin Jane at right.

CHAPTER 9

Pearl Harbor: Early 1941

Arizona, one of the Navy's main battlewagons, was the flagship of Admiral Isaac C. Kidd's flotilla, Battleship Division One, home ported at Pearl Harbor, Territory of Hawaii. Battleship Division One consisted of the flagship USS *Arizona* (fig. 9-1), and battleships USS *Nevada* (fig. 9- 2) and USS *Pennsylvania* (fig. 9-3). Tom was the fleet chaplain again, pastor to his shipmates. At the time, the ships of Division One were among the most modern and powerful battleships in the fleet. Figure 9-4 shows the ship as she had looked earlier in time, still equipped with the basket weave towers. These were later removed and replaced with sturdier tripod masts to hold the gunnery spotters' stations at the top. One reason for this redesign was that in rough seas, the crewmen manning these maintop stations were whipped about mercilessly due to the flexibility of the structure. Figure 9-1 shows what the ship looked like after the conversion.

In 1940, the United States was deeply concerned about the military activities of the Empire of Japan in Asia. While Japan had built a significant naval power and presence in the Asian arena, the United States Navy's Pacific Fleet was considered the most formidable fighting force in the Pacific basin; one for which the Japanese Navy would be no match. Indeed, many in the U.S. Navy believed that Japanese seamanship was not good enough for them to seriously consider crossing the vast Pacific Ocean to launch an attack on American territory. History shows this was an error of judgment and hubris that later proved fatal. The Pacific Fleet had been home ported on the West Coast but, just in case, was moved to Pearl Harbor specifically to provide the nation with advance warning and defense capability should Japan, against all odds, decide to strike at the United States. No one seriously expected the tragic events about to unfold.

Earlier, in a letter to Genevieve from the aircraft carrier USS *Saratoga*, Tom had expressed a marked preference for duty aboard a battleship.

> *These three days have been busy ones for the ship. Flight operations each morning and endless shifting of planes about on the flight deck and in and out of the hangar deck during the afternoon and evening. I begin to realize how truly Askin spoke when he said this was a "working" ship. A battleship can't compare with it.*

He was referring to Chaplain Askin, his immediate predecessor aboard *Saratoga*. Again later, he wrote:

> *Last night we had a smoker, and I was mighty glad when it was all over in a fairly successful way. Our men didn't come out well in the bouts we arranged with fighters from the* Mississippi, *but all in all it was quite a successful affair. I'm told that it was the first evening smoker ever held on the flight deck here, which perhaps accounts for the fact that I couldn't find anyone who knew just how to arrange for it. I learned a lot. And I'm more than ever convinced that the battleship chaplains don't know what real hard work is in such affairs. I can see some reasons why I'd prefer a battlewagon for my next sea duty.*

In those days, the era of naval air power was just beginning, and the battleship still reigned in the minds of many as the supreme expression of naval power.

Genevieve and Tommy moved back to Southern California and began looking for suitable quarters in Long Beach while Tom accompanied the ship to Pearl Harbor. The house-hunting process wasn't as easy in this Navy town as in Bremerton. Tommy transferred briefly to a local public school, then to the private Chadwick Seaside School. On April 4, Tom wrote:

Dearest:

... So, you haven't moved, I thought you had a definite place picked out from what you said in the letter just before this one. I agree with you that you can't be happy if you have to keep Tommy tied down too tight, a boy just can't stand it. I didn't realize that the school was so expensive, but it is probably worth it under the circumstances. As for our own immediate future plans, I hope that Bob will write promptly what he plans to do with the four of us selected to Captain who are now simply ship's chaplains. I look to see Maquire stay on for a time, and perhaps Ackiss, as both are Force chaplains. Did you mention extra money? Say, there won't be much ...

There is a lot going on in this letter. Genevieve had problems locating acceptable housing, and Tommy's public school experience proved unsatisfactory to her, hence the move to the relatively expensive, but far superior, Chadwick. In addition to the problems on the home front, Tom had just been selected for promotion to captain, an event that was cause for a great outpouring of congratulations from his brethren in the Chaplain Corps, reflected in the many letters he received at the time. All was not celebration, however, as Tom alluded to in his reference to his classmate and friend, Chaplain Bob Workman, who at the time was chief of chaplains. In a later letter, Tom wrote of his great disappointment that Chaplain Workman seemed disinclined to reassign chaplains who had attained the rank of captain to shore duty. Tom felt they could have a wider impact ashore than they could aboard a single ship. In addition, in one more example of the difficulties families encountered in the military life, Tom was forced to disappoint Genevieve's hope that the promotion would make their financial situation significantly easier.

On April 13, Easter Sunday, Tom wrote:

Dearest:

Here's hoping that you are enjoying beautiful Easter weather as we are, for this is one of those perfect days that Hawaii boasts about.... Got back in good time for my own service, which I found beautifully rigged, with two vases of lilies on the altar and seating for about 150. So many came that extra chairs and mess benches had to be brought, probably had about 200 present. For Communion there remained 107 who partook. So it has been a blessed Easter thus far.... We are moored alongside the USS Nevada, *and Ray Drinan said that at seven this evening they would stage an hour's entertainment, facing the* Arizona *so that all our men could enjoy it also. The next few days promise to be busy ones on board, as the fleet is taking the international situation very seriously and is making every possible preparation for developments. As indeed we have been doing for several months. I wish that the labor unions could only wake up to the present crisis and cooperate.*

The fleet had been conducting intensive training exercises at sea for some months in expectation of war. Tom's comment about labor unions reflects the fact that the 1930s were tumultuous times in American labor. There was a great deal of union activity, met sometimes with violent corporate response, such as the notorious attack on union organizers by the Ford Motor Company. As soon as war broke out, Walter Reuther, head of the powerful United Auto Workers, made a no-strike pledge for the duration, and he was able to enforce it with his members.

On April 26, Tom sent a disconsolate letter to Genevieve, with bad news, confirming his earlier worries about Chaplain Workman's intentions.

After I had sent my last letter Thursday, we got the regular mail from Wednesday's steamer, and it had very disappointing word in it, which you'll want to know. In other words, I heard from Bob Workman, and he says that promotion to captain isn't going to make any difference in our sea duty at all, at all, and that we'll stay right where we are until we complete the normal tour at sea. I must confess that I've been pretty low-spirited ever since, for I had counted on getting ashore this summer. I can't see any logic in keeping senior chaplains at sea when we are developing great stations of several thousand men in various places of the U.S., where such chaplains would be of most value, if experience counts for anything. So I'm downhearted and disappointed. He said that this was the policy of the Bureau, by which I don't know whether it is something that has been talked over by the line or whether it is his policy as chief of the Chaplain's Division. Certainly the senior line officers afloat expected that chaplains who were selected for captain would go ashore,

*for both the admiral and the captain asked me a
few days after the word came out, whether I had
any idea where I'd be ordered. But, there's no use
worrying about it. As for family plans, I'm all at
sea. If I had any good reason to believe that the
ship would be back in the Navy Yard any time this
summer, I'd not even think of your coming out
here. But no one seems to know, or if so, they
don't say, and one or two of the wives arrive
every couple of weeks. Eventually they find places
to live, though several are going over to the other
side of the island.*

On May 1, in a much better mood, Tom wrote to
Tommy describing a bit of the lighter side of life aboard a
battleship.

*Last night we had a hula show on board the ship,
and you would have enjoyed that also. For the
big, fat woman sang some very funny songs, and
danced as a fat woman would, and the real hula
girls (five of them) gave beautiful dances with
gourds in their hands as rattles, and bamboo
wands, and flattened round rocks which they
clicked together. The part everyone enjoyed most
was when the big woman came down off the
stage and invited the admiral to hula with her,
and he did it. That showed he was a good sport,
for an admiral is an important person, and
dignified, and when he does something like this it
shows that he enjoys fun and will help make fun
for everyone; it is liked by everyone. I surely enjoy
your letters, so write often.*

Your loving Dad

Tom, in addition to describing the event, was also
giving Tommy a lesson in leadership. Both *Arizona's*

skipper, Captain Van Valkenburgh, and division commandant, Admiral Kidd, were well-liked by the crew, for reasons Tom tried to illustrate to Tommy.

In a letter to Genevieve on May 8, Tom talked about some of the responsibilities he carried out as the *Arizona's* chaplain.

> *Yesterday was taken up with a trip around the island with two busloads from the ship. I marvel at how seldom some of the men go ashore. Half the crowd had never got as far as Waikiki Beach, and one or two hadn't been ashore in Honolulu at all.*

Herb Buehl, a crewman aboard *Arizona*, sent a photograph he had taken of the chaplain, who he knew well, to Tommy many years later (fig. 9-5). It shows Tom in a role he had fulfilled many times before in his career as a ship's chaplain, escorting a group of seamen as he described in his letter. They are shown here stopping at a famous overlook point on the mountainous Kolekole Highway on Oahu. Also in this letter, Tom commented on one of the most important responsibilities of a ship's chaplain: acting as a sort of father figure and counselor to the men of the crew.

> *... Today, all day on board, getting mail ready, and talking to various men who wanted to see me. A steady stream of family or personal problems, though not so many as at MCB SD.*

In the same letter, Tom refers to one of the social responsibilities that fell to wives of chaplains. Genevieve was expected to keep in touch with the families of Tom's fellow *Arizona* officers, as in his reference to the wife of Lt. Commander Fuqua in the next letter. Even though Fuqua was a junior officer, he proved a genuine hero during the Pearl Harbor attack. After all of the more senior officers aboard had been killed, he took command of the ship and calmly directed rescue operations as the ship was burning and sinking. He was credited with saving a number of his fellow crewmen's lives, at great risk to his own life, and as a result was awarded the Congressional Medal of Honor. Tom wrote:

> *I'm glad that you find Mrs. Fuqua so congenial, and I hope that you'll also like Mrs. Van Valkenburgh and her family, especially since they are so near. I'm not sure but that there's a grandson almost Tom's age.... These airmail exchanges make you seem nearer, and that's a fine feeling. You haven't mentioned your landlady lately, so I hope that all is happy in that respect. Are houses getting hard to find in Long Beach? San Diego is so bad that the C-in-C has issued a letter asking all personnel to warn their families not to go there unless they have living arrangements made in advance. Apparently a good many were going there in hopes of getting into the new Defense Housing Projects. Well, here's a heart full of love to you and Tom, sleeping by now, for it's almost twelve in L.B.*
>
> *Your loving Hubby*

Tom tried to celebrate Mother's Day, writing Genevieve a letter dated May 11, from the *Arizona*, which was in port for a short time. He had arranged with another chaplain to have flowers delivered to her for the occasion, and he enclosed a card (fig. 9-6).

> *Dear Mother:*
>
> *Put down that rolling pin! For this is Mother's Day, and I'm speaking for Tommy as well as myself. I hope that the flowers arrived in good order to bring you his Mother's Day greeting with mine.*

In the same letter, Tom mentioned another ship, the USS *Concord* (fig. 9-7), a light cruiser assigned to the Pacific Fleet and that had been taking part in the intensive training exercises off Hawaii.

> *The* Concord *has been to Samoa not long since, and from all indications it is a fast-changing place. They are building the USMC barracks in Hop Sing's valley, and meanwhile have temporary camp (apparently) in Utulei. "Red" said he enjoyed the visit greatly, but he didn't get any kava! Guess I'll have to go with the next ship and see that my friends have all the honors due.*

During the war, Samoa was used as a valuable and strategically located jumping off point for the fleet that was fighting its way island by island across the Pacific. As Tom noted, the island was already undergoing change in preparation for the coming war, a fact that probably bothered Tom since he admired the traditional Samoan culture so much. After the war, most Samoans no longer lived in the old way. Having been employed by the U.S. Navy, they were making good money and, for better or worse, were adopting the modern American lifestyle.

On May 20, Tom wrote Genevieve a long, newsy letter while *Arizona* was at sea. It included some remarks about the question troubling most of his fellow officers: should they or shouldn't they have their families come out to the islands?

> *A few minutes ago I was talking to Major Fox and Captain Shapley, and we agreed that we'd like to have our families here, but that we'd hate to have them on the way as we are going elsewhere. Did you hear what happened to Mrs. Fitz? She was all ready to start for Honolulu when she got a cablegram from him to start east, as he was*

sending that from Havana. No one seems to know just where the Yorktown *is; it has been three weeks since any of the families had word, so I understand, and we suspicion that she is on the Atlantic Coast. Of course we all expect that the battleships will remain in Hawaii, but who knows? Also, it might be that there will be some quick visits to Long Beach, and I believe that it is quite probable that we'll be in the Bremerton Yard some time this autumn, unless war actually breaks out. So I guess that we'll just have to wait a bit longer and see what develops. Do you agree?*

Your loving hubby,

Tom

On May 23, with *Arizona* back in port, Tom again wrote about the question proving so vexing: should Genevieve and Tommy move to the islands?

I don't want to decide the Honolulu question, and yet I suppose I'll have to help decide it. I really believe that for another sixty days it would be wise for any wife or family to remain in California rather than come to Honolulu. Especially if you can keep your comfortable place, and if Tommy is well, and so on. For I feel that the war situation is going to develop fast one way or another, and one can't tell what may take place under either circumstance. I'd hate to have you on the way, and me in the position of Hal Fitz.

This letter illustrates the tensions military families faced, feeling as though they were living under the Sword of Damocles and that it could descend at any moment. In spite of being physically separated, Tom made a concerted effort to make Tommy feel as though he still had a father. The same day, he wrote:

Dear Tom,

Well, how do you like this malahini (fig. 9-8)? Do you see what I am eating? Yes, it's your favorite, a vanilla ice cream cone. It was taken when I had a party of sixty sailors out on a sightseeing party the last time the ship was in port. I don't know whether I'll have a trip of this kind while we are here this time or not, for first we have three days of admiral's inspection, and then we paint the entire ship (at least the outside). Then we have three afternoons of baseball. After that I want to get up a big "smoker," with boxing and such things, as well as music and entertainment. You'll enjoy reading about our last "happy hour," held last Sunday, so I'll send you along a paper. I had a letter from Chaplain Truitt, who said that you were getting to be a much bigger boy than when you were in Bremerton, so hurry up and send me a snapshot to let me see just how big you have gotten in these four months since I saw you. And don't forget that I love a letter from you every now and then.

Your loving DAD

On June 6, Tom wrote Genevieve a letter with some good news for a change. He was coming home for a visit.

Dearest:

Well, here's some surprising news for you. Due to a very unexpected opportunity I'm booked for a visit to Long Beach June 17 to July 1. I can't tell you how I'm going to get there, but so far as human plans are certain, you can count on this. I probably won't have all that time for a trip, but at least can spend much of it with you and Tommy. So have the car put in shape for a good spin upon my arrival and lots of good times while I'm home.

Now there's another thing that I believe we ought to do if it is at all possible, and that is, arrange for Mother to visit us during that period. I've wished so many times that I had taken a trip to see her before the ship left, that I feel I mustn't fail to see her on this visit. But I don't want to fly east and back after a day or so, cutting down my visit with you and Tommy by that much, and the time is too short for all of us to take a train trip to Chestnut Hill, or even Denver. Denver would be possible, of course, but it is so unsatisfactory so far as Tommy is concerned. So all in all I believe that if Mary thinks Mother can stand the trip, she should come on to Long Beach. I don't know of any better way to use some or all of that savings account than this, for in these times, we need to take the opportunity when we have it. So you send on a check for whatever is needed, if you agree with me. I don't know whether we ought to suggest that Mary take the trip or not, you use your own judgment about that after you read Mary's letters which are in this mail.

The reason Tom couldn't tell Genevieve how he was going to get there was that it was the *Arizona* that was going to make a quick trip to the mainland. For security reasons, Naval personnel were probably cautioned not to make explicit references to ship movements, lest their letters fall into the wrong hands. At that time, the military were aware that there were agents of Japan on Oahu charting the comings and goings of the Naval vessels at Pearl Harbor. Tom's desire to have a visit with his mother proved prescient, since she died a short time later.

The same day, Tom sent a letter to Tommy telling him about a Samoan dance troupe he had arranged to give a performance aboard *Arizona.*

Dear Son Tom:

Thank you for the little boats and greyhound bus and even more for the good letters that came with them. You are getting to be an excellent correspondent. I wish you could have been here last night, for we had a group of Samoans on board, who gave us a program of siva siva, singing, basket weaving, and copra cutting. The man in charge used to teach in Poyer School. He was dressed as a talking chief, with his big "fui" (fly flapper of sennit) and staff. You remember the ones we picked up when we left San Diego, don't you? My staff had been cut in half so that it could go into the box. The girls had on lavalavas of Tahitian cloth, and wore girdles made of nuts, like the one you used to cavort about in. They also did several knife dances, with the big knives with hooked end, like ours except that these were made of steel. Toward the end they sang a Samoan hymn and asked anyone who recognized it to hold up his hand, and they gave the first one to do this a coconut frond basket and a coconut they had split open. I didn't recognize it at first, and then I suddenly realized that it was "What a friend we have in Jesus." About the same time several of the sailors also recognized it and held up their hands and got the prize. Then what do you suppose they sang as the final number on the program? Yes, you guessed it, "Good-bye, my faleni." I was glad they didn't use any grass skirts last night, for that's more Hawaiian than Samoan. So I imagined myself back in Samoa for that hour last night. As one part of the course, there were dozens of fish jumping out of the water, trying to get away from a larger fish, I suppose. If I could get on a magic carpet this morning I'd spend the day with you, but since I can't I will have to send my love to you in this letter.

Tofa, soifua,

Dad

The *Arizona* arrived in Long Beach on June 11, and Tom surprised Tommy at school. When Tommy saw his father approaching across the campus, he ran toward Tom, nearly knocking him flat by jumping full tilt into his arms.

On June 22, while Tom was enjoying time with his family, Germany invaded the Soviet Union, an action of enormous significance to the Japanese High Command. They believed it meant Japan would not have to contend with Soviet armed forces interfering with their imperialistic plans in Asia. They believed that the German juggernaut was going to easily crush the Soviets. As a result, Japan proceeded to invade all of Indo-China, an action that caused great consternation in the United States.

While these momentous events were taking place, Tom, Genevieve, and Tommy said good-bye after a visit altogether too short. Though they could not have known, it was the last time they would be together. *Arizona* left on her return trip to Pearl Harbor days before Tom's birthday on July 5.

Fig. 9-1 U.S.S. Arizona Flagship of Division One.

Fig. 9-2 U.S.S. Nevada of Division One.

Fig. 9-3 U.S.S. Pennsylvania of Division One

Fig. 9-4 U.S.S. Arizona Shown as she was configured at launch.

Fig. 9-5 At Kolekole Pass overlook

Fig. 9-6 Tom's 1941 Mother's Day Greeting to Genevieve

Fig. 9-7 U.S.S. Concord

Fig. 9-8 The "Malahini"

CHAPTER 10

Pearl Harbor: Late 1941

On July 10, having been forced to celebrate his birthday apart from his family, Tom wrote a disconsolate letter to Genevieve.

> *Dearest,*
>
> *I've just finished tearing up a letter I wrote to you and Tommy on my birthday. I was feeling pretty sorry for myself when I wrote it, and now that several days have gone by before the airmail was starting for the coast, I have decided that it should not be sent. So, you'll have to take the will for the deed, and if you want to, you can date this back to my natal day and know that I was thinking of you both, and wishing that I could be cutting a cake at home.*

And Tom was not the only one feeling blue. He went on to describe the rest of the crew as being in a down mood as the ship headed west for Hawaii.

> *I've never seen so quiet a ship as ours was for the first few days after we left, even on the Fourth I didn't stage a "happy hour" because several key men said that they thought the crew would rather loaf and sleep, and that suited me.*

Maybe the crew had a premonition that it might have been the last time they would ever see their loved ones. It also didn't help Tom's state of mind that he had just heard from his sister Mary. Her daughter Jane had developed a form of schizophrenia and was in the sanitarium undergoing treatment. He worried about the financial drain on Mary, and the emotional strain on both Mary and his mother. Tom closed the letter in a particularly heartfelt manner, saying:

> *I'm sending a world of love to you and Tommy. One thing I did say in my torn-up letter was that God had given me a wonderful wife and son.*
>
> *Worlds of love,*
>
> *Tom*

On July 22, Tom replied to Genevieve in a letter that may have sounded ominous to her since he discussed money matters and life insurance policies.

> *As for insurance loans, I'll send to the Presbyterian Ministers Fund and ask for a policy loan application on the oldest policy, and when that comes I'll fill it in and send it to you, so you can send it on with the policy in question if a loan becomes necessary. They charge only 4% interest, as against 5% on the Equitable. Also I will fill out the assignment forms so that you will have full power over both equitable policies, to borrow, cash in, or otherwise dispose of them. That's just to safeguard you against any sudden need for money with me where I couldn't help.*

He also revisited the ongoing question about whether she and Tommy should come to Hawaii.

*Now as to other questions you raised, I wish I
could feel sure what is the wise thing for you and
Tommy to do. Suppose we put off this decision for
another two weeks, maybe something will happen
to give us the final indication. At the present,
much as I'd like to have you here, I can't feel that
it would be best for the family. When I see what
folks live in, and at what cost, it just seems
foolish. Permanent residents can live happily here,
but most Navy families I don't believe are doing
so. And always the possibility of a yard period at
Bremerton sooner than we think.*

Three days later, the United States reacted to
Japan's provocative military moves in Indo-China by
imposing an oil embargo on Japan and by freezing all
Japanese assets in the U.S. The Japanese looked upon
this move as an existential threat to their continued
military expansion, and they began considering their
response. They had two choices: either try to repair the
tattered relationship between the two countries, or go to
war. After a heated debate, the Japanese High Command
made the fateful decision to go to war.

At that time Genevieve and Tommy had traveled by
the Southern Pacific's famous streamlined train, the *San
Joaquin Daylight,* to visit Tom's cousin Nita Kirkpatrick
Drees and her family in Vallejo, California. The Southern
Pacific right of way climbed over the Tehachapi
Mountains in Southern California, at one point traveling
around the famed Tehachapi Loop, a tight circle that
allowed the tracks to climb the steep mountain grade
without taking up as much linear distance. The front
end of a long train, such as the *Daylight,* passed over a
trestle just as the final few cars went under—a sight
Tommy would long remember. Genevieve continued
corresponding with Tom during the Vallejo visit.

He replied to one of her letters on July 24, writing from aboard the *Arizona*.

Dearest:

Your airmail from Vallejo arrived today, and was waiting for me when I arrived on board after taking another two busloads around the island. I'm sorry that you struck such a hot trip and hot spell at Vallejo. You must have taken the valley route, which can be terrific. I hope that the heat hasn't continued, and that you're even now enjoying a very delightful visit. Just where did Nita pack you all in?

... This will reach you about August 2 and will remind you that I haven't forgotten that anniversary. I wish that we could be together, but since we can't, I want you and Tommy to celebrate and tell me all about it later. If you liked perfume, and if I hadn't already brought you a bottle from here, I'd send you some. If you liked necklaces, and didn't already have a lot you never wear, I'd send you some. If you went in for sarongs and flowered silks, I might send you some. So what shall I do! I guess just send you worlds of love and mountains of good birthday wishes.

Your loving Tom

And, once again, the ever-present war worries came to the surface in a letter Tom wrote to Genevieve on July 31.

Dearest,

This may not be much of a letter, for I'm tired and out of sorts, and that isn't a good start for a conversation or letters either. It has been a peculiar week. Possibly the situation in the Orient also has us a bit uneasy and on a strain, although this evening's newscast seems to indicate no immediate trouble, by which I mean actual warfare. It's a sorry old world right now, isn't it?

Greatly as I wish that you and Tommy could be here with me, I still feel that it would be ill-advised right now, both because of the family situation and because of the war situation. But, if you have meanwhile decided otherwise, just let me know and I'll meet the steamer or have someone do it for me.... As I interpreted your letter, you wouldn't be leaving for St. Louis until August 15 at the earliest. Worlds of love to you and to Tommy. What I wouldn't give to be coming home each evening after the day's work was ended and living life as it was intended to be lived. Well, the months will pass, and one of these days we'll have some shore duty again.

All my love,

Tom

Tom and Genevieve had decided that she and Tommy would move to St. Louis, far away from the feared Japanese invasion point and a city where she had a number of close family members she could rely on.

On August 2, Genevieve's birthday, Tom's letter was full of love and happy birthday wishes as well as some practical directives in regard to the insurance policies.

Dearest,

If you have thought of me as many times as I have thought of you, then I've been with you often as the day has come and gone. I hope that you received the roses I sent to you today. They were to be a little reminder of my love on your birthday. And I hope that you and Tommy had some sort of celebration.... The next steamer mail leaves Wednesday, August 8. On that I'm sending you the power-of-attorney, or rather the assignment, of the Equitable Policies. Will send some directions about this at the time. Sent the U.S. Government policy by registered mail Friday. This assignment will have to be attached to the policies, which are in the safety deposit box. I have an idea you'll want to have all these papers in a safety deposit box in St. Louis.... Well, my dearest, I didn't intend this to be anything but a love letter, but I see I've dropped in some business. I haven't typed this, but I hope you can read it anyhow.

Bushels of love,

Tom

Tucked into the envelope with the letter was a short handwritten note (fig. 10-1) that expressed Tom's love even more succinctly. Genevieve kept this note for the rest of her life.

August brought scorching, muggy weather to Hawaii, and those who had to endure it aboard ship felt the heat even worse than those on land. Tom wrote in a letter on August 8:

We have been having some of the weather we used to get in Samoa, very humid and little breeze. That's bad on board ship, for we just keep getting hotter and hotter until sundown, and then cool off very slowly.

However, in the same letter, he tried to banish the blues by saying:

Whenever I begin to feel sorry for myself at not seeing you and Tommy, and for you not having me home (conceit), I think of what some British officers told us the other day: they hadn't seen their families for more than a year, and didn't know when they would. That's sea service for you. So I wipe out my own self-pity by thinking of that kind of duty, which probably is quite common for the British these last two years. I hope that we won't have to get any like it.

Well, here's a hug and a kiss and worlds of love to you and to Tommy as well.

Dad

During this time period, the Japanese High Command, who had already determined that war was the preferred option, considered Admiral Yamamoto's bold plan to attack the American fleet in Pearl Harbor. There were a number of dissenters who felt it was too risky, and they argued that another plan could be devised with lower risk. Yamamoto, convinced that the American fleet had to be destroyed before Japan embarked on any other military moves, meanwhile had gone ahead with his planning and preparation. Two critical elements of their Naval Air armaments needed improvement. The otherwise accurate Japanese long-range torpedoes had to be modified so they could be air dropped and not hit the bottom in the relatively shallow Pearl Harbor waters. They had to design armor-piercing bombs to penetrate the deck armor of the American ships as well as reach far enough below deck to do maximum damage when they exploded. While he was successfully directing these improvements, he continued arguing for his plan, against powerful opposition. He finally got it approved, only by threatening to resign from his position as commander in chief of the Japanese Combined Fleet.

On August 8, Tom wrote a letter to his sister Mary.

Dear Mary:

... Yes, I wish that it were possible for us to be near you now, but so far as I can foresee, I'll be at sea for another year. And being at sea will probably mean being out in the Pacific, probably basing on Hawaii as we have been doing for sixteen months. I hope you won't be misled by such newscasts as we heard the day the Japs moved South, that the "Fleet had steamed out of Pearl Harbor under sealed orders," all of which was nonsense. As a matter of fact, all ships move under secret orders these days, and we are constantly coming and going in and out of Pearl Harbor, some in and others out, but it doesn't mean what the newscast implied. So don't get worried at such things. If true, worry wouldn't help, but they probably won't be true if you do hear them. Which isn't to say that we wouldn't all love to be back in California waters, for this tourist paradise when viewed in short periods from a beach and a wide veranda, is anything but that when viewed over a period of months from a ship with steel sides that absorb all the heat during the day and don't cool off until morning.

I don't know exactly what Genevieve has decided to do, for she was up with Nita when she wrote me last, some days ago. Since that the Oriental situation has become definitely more serious, and our own movements are not any more certain than they were, and it seems rather foolish for her and Tommy to come to Hawaii at considerable expense, live in inferior quarters at about double the cost, and perhaps wake up one day to learn that the reason I didn't come home when I thought

I'd return is that the ship went to Bremerton Navy Yard for a month or two. All of which might easily happen. It seems so much more sensible to forego family life for a time, and for Tommy to get in a steady year of school in St. Louis. But I dare say, she has written you, and that perhaps you know more of her present plans than I do at the moment. I feel sure that a letter has gone astray.

I know that you don't feel like writing to anyone, Mary, but I do hope you'll drop us a line frequently, for we are anxious to know just how both of you [Mary and Jane] are. With a heart full of love,

Your brother

On August 29, Tom's commission as regular captain finally arrived. He had been serving as ad interim captain since July 1, and he had been anxiously awaiting his permanent commission.

On September 6, the Japanese High Command made the decision to go with Yamamoto's plan for making war on the United States. Preparations then began in earnest, using Kagoshima Bay on the Japanese home island of Kyushu because of its close similarity to the topography of Pearl Harbor. Naval pilots practiced endlessly, learning how to drop the modified torpedoes with great accuracy in the restricted drop zone. High altitude bomber pilots practiced dropping the new armor-piercing bombs from the precise altitude needed to pierce deck armor, without at the same time penetrating too many decks below to be maximally effective. Finally, Yamamoto was ready, but he lacked final authority to launch his strike.

On October 19, Tom wrote a letter to Genevieve in St. Louis. He speculated once again about conditions around the world, and how they might affect America and his possibility of shore duty.

Your question about my conversation with Charlotte Masterson, it made me no happier to be alone and to have you and Tommy so far away, but it did sort of confirm my feeling that we did the right thing. I find that there's a difference of opinion among seniors as to the possible or probable effect of recent Russian-German-Japanese actions. My admiral said he thought we weren't any nearer actual hostilities out here and that present routine would continue. But Captain V. said he was preparing for a move any day anywhere and would be surprised at nothing. Well, I'll be glad when Maguire gets back and some definite word is at hand about myself, for I still think some sort of change will be made in spite of what Bob wrote. Of course, I may be entirely wrong. I'm glad to note that you are getting into the church life of the community, and hope that you're going to find enough community interests, and Tommy also, to keep you happy this winter. After all, time is passing and shore duty gets closer with each week.

He closed on a hopeful note:

The rain has given way to lovely sunshine this morning, and I wish that you and Tommy could enjoy it with me. But one of these days, the Lord willing, we will be together again. Sunday morning greetings and love to both of my dear ones way back in St. Louis.

Tom

It was at this critical time that Tom's beloved mother passed away suddenly in the home she shared in Pennsylvania with his sister Mary. Tom had been exceptionally close to his mother, so the news left him disconsolate. On October 28, a heartbroken Tom wrote to his sister Bertha.

Dear Bertha:

You probably wonder why I didn't sit down and write you at once upon getting word about Mother's death, but the truth is I have been so broken up that I haven't been able to write anyone. I started a letter to you on Monday, but gave it up when I saw that I couldn't make a go of it. All the letters from the East had been so cheerful, and Mother had been so well that I wasn't prepared at all for this. Nor were you, I expect. In a letter from Mary on October 6, she says Mother had a slight heart attack, but the next day was busy putting up jelly. So I guess it came as she would have had it, with the end in a few hours. I am so sorry that I can't be there. But the expense would be too great for what little I can do, and so I am not trying to do it at all. I know that Mother would rather have me remember her as I last saw her, waving goodbye at Denver. Genevieve is sending flowers for us, and I hope you will put them on with my love and affection. The Navy is a cruel taskmaster at times, for I have been far away at the funeral of Dad, Gladys, and now Mother. Write and tell me about everything, won't you, Bertha. And tell Mary that I sent her a letter on Monday, the only one I was able to write, and that not very legible.

My love is with you, Bertha, for I know you are feeling this most keenly. And tell Aunt Anna she has my love and sympathy too.

Your brother,

Roy

On November 3 in Japan, the chief of the Naval General Staff had approved Yamamoto's plan to launch the attack on Pearl Harbor early in December. They planned to attack early on a Sunday morning. The Japanese understood that Americans let their guard down on Sundays, thinking about church attendance and other peaceful pursuits. Yamamoto's forces began their final preparations and stood by for the order to set sail.

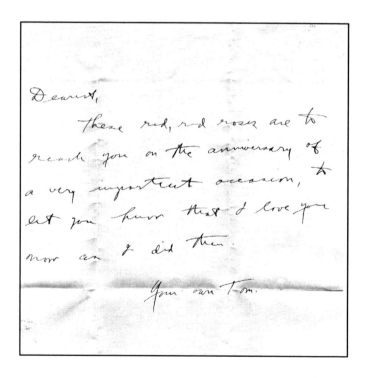

Fig. 10-1 Tom's Wedding Anniversary note to Genevieve in 1941

CHAPTER 11

Countdown to Infamy

On November 26, Tom wrote a letter to Genevieve hinting at a possible visit to Long Beach by *Arizona*, allowing the family to be together again for a short while. He had to use circumspect language since the situation with Japan had continued to grow increasingly negative. The Navy knew the fleet was being carefully watched for any sign of a significant movement that Japanese agents around Pearl Harbor might interpret as a signal of deployment to Asian waters, thereby threatening Japan's war plans there.

Dearest:

Just a short letter tonight, as there's airmail leaving tomorrow, and I want to get this on it. You should have had my letter of the twenty-second, with its good news, by this time. Nothing further. Dr. Johnson and one or two others are the only ones who know it for the present. I still think that the Lafayette Hotel will be the place to rendezvous, no matter where we stay.... I'm feeling better, and expect by the time I get to Long Beach to be on my toes. Had a letter from Tommy, and it was some letter. Do you see them before they are mailed, or does he do it all on his own! He didn't mention receiving the book; did it come all right? I hope so, for I put three dollars in it to buy you some flowers. Just a little reminder that I still love you. I hope that the Thanksgiving Day was a success and that you didn't have to be carried home from overeating. I didn't get anything for the men of the family except young George, so you get them something for us, especially the youngest member.

With love and everything, to both of you.

Tom

That same day Vice-Admiral Nagumo's carrier attack force sailed from Japanese waters, bound for Hawaii by a circuitous route across the far northern reaches of the Pacific Ocean, hoping to evade detection. Japan had committed all six of its most powerful aircraft carriers: *Akagi, Kaga, Soryu, Hiryu, Shokaku*, and *Zuikaka*. This formidable fleet, the most powerful carrier attack force ever assembled, consisted of:

6 aircraft carriers

2 battleships

2 heavy cruisers

1 light cruiser

9 destroyers

8 tankers

23 fleet submarines

5 midget submarines

414 aircraft

Radio silence was strictly enforced in hopes that American and British monitoring stations would be stymied in their efforts to locate the Japanese fleet, a hope that succeeded.

In Washington, D.C., Secretary of State Cordell Hull had been engaged in intense negotiations with the Japanese envoy, Saburo Kurusu, but to no avail. On

November 27, messages were sent from Washington to Pearl Harbor commanders, Admiral Husband E. Kimmel and General Walter C. Short, as well as to commanders in the Philippines. These messages were blunt warnings that war appeared not just inevitable but imminent. Though Washington could not pinpoint exactly where the Japanese attack would occur, the American High Command fully expected local commanders such as Kimmel and Short to immediately go on High Alert and deploy their forces accordingly. Why this did not happen has been investigated, discussed, and exhaustively written about elsewhere, most notably in Henry C. Clausen's authoritative book, *Pearl Harbor: Final Judgement* [sic]. The sad fact is that Kimmel and Short did not order a response, so the fleet lay defenseless on the morning of December 7.

On November 30, two events occurred. The final brick was laid in the Japanese attack plan when Emperor Hirohito finally gave his formal consent to go to war against America. Also on that day, an amazing news article was published. None other than Japanese Prime Minister General Hideki Tojo issued a blunt statement, published in the *New York Herald Tribune*, warning that Japan intended to "purge East Asia of US-British power with a vengeance." On the same day, the banner headlines in the *Honolulu Advertiser* read, "Kurusu Bluntly Warned Nation Ready for Battle" (fig. 11-1). Events began moving rapidly.

The next day the Japanese government gave formal approval of the plan to wage war. The Japanese attack force had made steady progress toward their objective, still undetected, and was now north of Hawaii. However, they still needed the final order to attack. On December 2, that order came in the form of a coded message radioed to Admiral Nagumo aboard his flagship, *Akagi* (fig. 11-2): "Climb Mount Niitaka." The point of no return had been reached and the countdown had begun.

On December 5, the Japanese fleet, fortuitously concealed under heavy cloud cover, refueled from the accompanying tankers in preparation for the attack. Admiral Nagumo then proceeded to his attack position, reaching a point approximately three hundred miles north of Oahu on December 6. Death was hours away for the men and ships of the United States Pacific Fleet. Before dawn on Sunday, December 7, aircraft of the first wave took off from the decks of the Japanese carrier task force and flew toward Oahu, following a signal from a Honolulu radio station as their directional guide.

That morning, Tom's alarm clock woke him around 6:45 so he would have time to prepare for the morning's Church Call. After breakfast he proceeded to the ship's afterdeck and began rigging for church under the large canvas awning erected there to shade the congregation from the intense tropical sun. It was a calm and beautiful morning as Tom worked, and he probably thought nothing of hearing aircraft droning in the distance toward the harbor. Other crewmen thought it was Army aircraft from nearby Hickam Field engaged in yet another early morning training mission. Shortly before 8:00 a.m., the first wave of attacking aircraft swept over Pearl Harbor, raining death and destruction on the totally unprepared Americans. As soon as the "meatball" insignia became visible to the crew of *Arizona*, the air raid alarm sounded. Tom abandoned his church preparations and started moving toward his battle station, sick bay, where his duties were to assist in treating the wounded and to minister to the dying.

At that moment, Boatswains Mate Second Class Thomas W. Stanborough was rushing to man his battle station, and he saw the chaplain moving forward from the ship's stern. As he described in his letter of condolence to Genevieve in 1943:

I am a survivor off the Arizona, *and I knew Captain Kirkpatrick, our chaplain, very well. He was a grand person, and I had often thought of contacting you, but never knew your address. I am sorry to say that I had not seen him after the bombing, but had seen him at the time of the alarm. He was on the stern rigging and preparing for church. That is how he died. He died serving God and his country.*

A moment later, a bomb dropped from one of the high-altitude bombers glanced off the number four turret closest to the ship's stern, exploded, and started a fire. Moments later, another high-altitude bomber dropped a 1700-pound armor-piercing bomb that penetrated the deck armor near the number two turret and exploded four decks below, igniting the forward magazine in a horrific explosion that literally tore the ship apart, killing 1,177 of the crew (Chapter 1, fig. 1-4). Witnesses around Pearl Harbor that day said, "No one who heard that sound will ever forget it."

Casualties included Captain Franklin Van Valkenburgh and Admiral Isaac C. Kidd. Both were killed on the bridge when they were engulfed by the intense fireball resulting from the detonation of so many tons of high explosive. Among the few survivors, Lt. Commander Samuel G. Fuqua, as the senior surviving officer aboard, took charge of rescue operations. One of those rescued was Seaman Herb Buell, whose battle station was in the number four turret. As he reported, he and the rest of the gunnery crew in the turret survived the initial explosion but found they were unable to breathe. The explosion had immediately consumed all the oxygen from the between- deck spaces, including the interior of the turret. Struggling for air, he and his comrades were able to climb into the counterbalance overhang at the rear of the turret, open a hatch, and drop to the deck below. From there Buell escaped to Ford Island.

The ship continued to burn for three days after the attack, spreading flaming fuel oil over the surface of Pearl Harbor, making the escape of those who survived the blast nearly impossible without suffering major burns. This news image (fig. 11-3) became the iconic symbol of the attack that roused and outraged the American people. It changed the largely pacifist and anti-interventionist sentiment of the people into a deep anger and a steely resolve that drove the greatest military buildup in history.

In the final few days of his life, Tom's activities had continued pretty much as usual. He worked on his Divine Worship Service plan for December 7, finished his sermon, planned the music program, and had the Order of Worship program printed. Still anticipating a reunion with Genevieve and Tommy, he wrote one last letter to Genevieve, dated December 4, 1941.

> *Dearest:*
>
> *Still nothing definite, but don't do anything until I write you. The Jap situation is so uncertain that anything can happen. I have just had a "booster" typhoid shot and a tetanus inoculation, pretty sore arm for a while. Everyone gets them. So be glad you aren't "in the Navy." Have about finished addressing the Christmas cards, and have written several notes as I've been reminded of folks whom I haven't written for a long time, so my record is better than for …*

The letter arrived in St. Louis a few days after the attack. This torn scrap is all that remains.

Genevieve found in the envelope a copy of Tom's Order of Services (fig. 11-4, 11-5) for the Divine Services he had intended to conduct that Sunday morning. While the service was oriented toward the Christmas season, it was prescient in several ways. He used as a prayer the hymn known throughout the English-speaking world as "The Navy Hymn," with its concluding stanzas: "Oh, hear us when we cry to Thee, for those in peril on the sea." Who knows what was going through his mind when out of the hundreds of Christmas carols he could have chosen the one he picked was the hymn "Watchman, Tell Us of the Night." While it is a traditional Christmas carol, the title fairly defines the reason the Pacific Fleet was stationed in Hawaii: to be the watchman for the nation should Japan launch an attack on the United States across the Pacific. On the back of the program, Tom placed a poem by Rev. William Wood with closing lines: "You'll find a Presence by you in the furnace, You'll find a Presence by you on the Sea, You'll find a Presence by you in the Battle, Yes, Everywhere and Always Victory!" There seems little doubt that he intended to offer inspiration and comfort to the men of the *Arizona* in anticipation of coming battles during which many would suffer and some would perish. Tragically the final battle arrived for the men of the USS *Arizona* before their chaplain had the chance to deliver these uplifting messages on that peaceful Sunday morning in Hawaii.

THE END

Fig. 11-1 Newspaper headline warned of attack a week earlier

Fig. 11-2 Admiral Nagumo's flagship Akagi

Fig. 11-3 The Iconic news photo of Arizona burning Galvanized American people.

IF

"If you can go to Church when all about you
Are going everywhere but to the House of
   Prayer,
If you can travel straight when others wobble
And do not seem to have a righteous care,
If you can teach and not get tired of teaching,
Or tell the truth when others lie like sin,
Or pray and pay and carry heavy burdens
Without a murmur, Brother, you will win!

If you possess yourself and pray 'God bless
   you!'
When every muscle in you aches to smite,
When something says, 'Give up! Give up the
   struggle!
Since others fail why stand alone and fight '
You'll find a Presence by you in the furnace,
You'll find a Presence by you on the sea,
You'll find a Presence by you in the battle,
Yes, Everywhere and always victory!"

—Rev. William Wood.

DIVINE SERVICES

on board

UNITED STATES SHIP ARIZONA

December 7, 1941

Third Sunday before Christmas

Church Call at 1000

Catholic Church Party
to U.S.S. Nevada, 0930

Organ Music by Transcription at 0945

Fig. 11-4 Order of Worship Intended to be celebrated on December 7, 1941.

ORDER OF SERVICES

Prelude.. Ship's Band

The Call to Worship

Doxology.. Hymn 252

Invocation, concluding with the Lord's Prayer

Prayer Hymn.............Without Announcement

Scripture Lesson ....Acts 28:11-31

Morning Prayer

Hymn.. No. 45
   "Watchman, Tell Us of the Night"

Sermon ...."Rome and Bethlehem"

Hymn "From the Eastern Mountains" No. 43

The Benediction

Band Postlude

Prayer Hymn

"Eternal Father, strong to save,
Whose arm doth bind the restless wave;
Who bidds't the mighty ocean deep
Its own appointed limits keep;
O hear us when we cry to Thee
For those in peril on the sea.—Amen."

Fig. 11-5 Order of Worship inside

Epilogue

Writing this account of my parents' life together as a military family has been an intensely personal experience. What follows below may help to explain why. On May 30, 2011, I wrote a letter to the editors of our local newspaper, the *San Jose Mercury News*. I was responding to a Memorial Day column authored by journalist Kimberly Hefling, which was published on the Op Ed page the previous day. In my letter, I made the following observations.

Kimberly Hefling's thoughtful and poignant article about the children of fallen warriors touches on a subject I believe American national leaders need to think deeply about. From personal experience I think I am entitled to speak with some authority. My father, Chaplain Thomas LeRoy Kirkpatrick, gave his life for his country on December 7, 1941, aboard the USS Arizona *at Pearl Harbor, along with most of his shipmates. I know it might be difficult for most Americans to truly appreciate what it does to a child when a warrior parent is suddenly and brutally torn from him or her. In the article, Hefling quotes young Danielle Miller's reply to those who ask questions about her father, killed in Iraq. She tells them, "It's OK, I've learned to deal with it."*

Most of us do indeed learn to "deal" with it. However, that most emphatically does not mean we ever cease longing for our missing parent. Believe me, we don't. I was a young boy when my father died. Now I am an old man. Even so, after all these years, not a day goes by in which I don't miss my father and wonder how different my own life might have been had I grown up with his loving guidance and example.

I am not one of those who say we must never go to war again. God willing, we won't have to. But if it ever comes to that, my fervent prayer is that our national leaders, before taking us to war, count the true cost to be paid. It is not just the number of body bags sent home from the war zone, or the billions spent on war material, as important as these are. Rather, it must include the great and lifelong cost to the severely wounded, and to the survivors of the fallen warriors, especially their children.

But, there is more to this story. By the time I had reached middle age, I had visited the USS *Arizona* Memorial several times and had purchased and read a number of books about the attack. One day I happened to be rummaging around in some boxes of papers and mementoes my mother had passed on to me. There were letters, pictures, and one object wrapped up in several layers of heavy brown paper. I unwrapped it to discover a small desk alarm clock in deteriorating condition. It was the clock my mother had given my father, which he carried with him aboard the *Arizona*. I remembered having seen it on a couple of earlier occasions when my mother had taken it out to show me.

However, this time was different. Having become much better informed about the attack, particularly its timing, I saw something I had never noticed before. The hands of the clock were frozen at 8:05, the exact moment the ship was destroyed. This stark recognition made me feel suddenly and powerfully connected to the moment of

Father's death, as though I had traveled back in time to December 7, 1941, and watched it happen. I was so overcome with sudden grief that I could not speak. After a while, I carefully rewrapped the clock, wondering if others might react similarly. That's when I decided to donate the clock to the USS *Arizona* Memorial Museum where it is displayed to this day.

Thomas I. Kirkpatrick

CPSIA information can be obtained at www.ICGtesting.com
Printed in the USA
BVOW040658281011

274660BV00001B/3/P